Perfect practice for all the Year 4 Maths basics!

This superb CGP Foundation Targeted Question Book is perfect
for helping pupils get to grips with Maths in Year 4.

There's a huge range of questions on all the most important Maths skills,
carefully written to build pupils' confidence. Answers are included at the back.

And there's more! We've included practice tests at the start and end
of the book — ideal for keeping track of progress. Enjoy!

What CGP is all about

Our sole aim here at CGP is to produce the highest quality
books — carefully written, immaculately presented and
dangerously close to being funny.

Then we work our socks off to get them out to you
— at the cheapest possible prices.

Contents

About This Book 1

Year Three Objectives Test 2

Section One – Number and Place Value

Counting in Multiples 6
Counting Backwards Through Zero 7
Place Value and Partitioning 8
1000 More or Less 9
Ordering and Comparing Numbers 10
Rounding 12
Decimal Numbers and Fractions 14
Roman Numerals 15
Solving Number Problems 16

Section Two – Calculations

Written Addition 18
Written Subtraction 19
Estimating and Checking 20
Using Times Tables 22
Mental Multiplying and Dividing 23
Factor Pairs 24
Written Multiplication 25
Solving Calculation Problems 26

Section Three – Fractions and Decimals

Counting in Hundredths 28
Equivalent Fractions 29
Adding and Subtracting Fractions 30
Fractions of Amounts 32
Decimals 34
Writing Fractions as Decimals 35
Dividing by 10 and 100 36
Rounding Decimals 38
Comparing Decimals 39
Solving Fraction and Decimal Problems 40

Section Four – Measurement

Units 42
Perimeter 44
Area 46
Money 48
Clocks 50
Time Problems 51

Section Five – Geometry

Comparing 2D Shapes 52
Comparing Angles 54
Finding Lines of Symmetry 56
Completing Symmetrical Shapes 57
Coordinates 58
Translations 59
Drawing Shapes on Grids 60

Section Six – Statistics

Bar Charts 61
Time Graphs 62
Interpreting Charts and Graphs 64

Year Four Objectives Test 67

Answers 71

Published by CGP

Editors:
Martha Bozic, Katie Fernandez, Rachel Hickman, Duncan Lindsay, Ali Palin, Tamara Sinivassen.

ISBN: 978 1 78908 044 5

With thanks to Samuel Mann for the proofreading.
With thanks to Emily Smith for the copyright research.

Printed by Sterling, Kettering.

Clipart from Corel®

Based on the classic CGP style created by Richard Parsons.

Text, design, layout and original illustrations © Coordination Group Publications Ltd. (CGP) 2022

All rights reserved.

Photocopying this book is not permitted, even if you have a CLA licence.
Extra copies are available from CGP with next day delivery • 0800 1712 712 • www.cgpbooks.co.uk

About This Book

This Book is Full of Year 4 Maths Questions

You'll learn a lot of <u>new maths</u> in Year 4.

This <u>foundation</u> book has questions on <u>all the maths</u> for Year 4 at a slightly <u>easier</u> level — so it's perfect if you're <u>getting to grips</u> with the Year 4 topics.

It <u>matches</u> our <u>Year 4 Study Book</u>. This can help you if you get stuck.

The <u>answers</u> to all of the questions are at the <u>back of this book</u>.

> This book covers the <u>Attainment Targets</u> for <u>Year 4</u> of the <u>National Curriculum</u>.

There are Two Objectives Tests in This Book

The one at the <u>front of the book</u> is to test that you <u>remember</u> the maths you learnt in <u>Year 3</u>.

The test at the <u>back of the book</u> is to see how well you know the maths in <u>this book</u>.

The questions in each test cover a <u>mix of different topics</u> and get trickier as you work through the test.

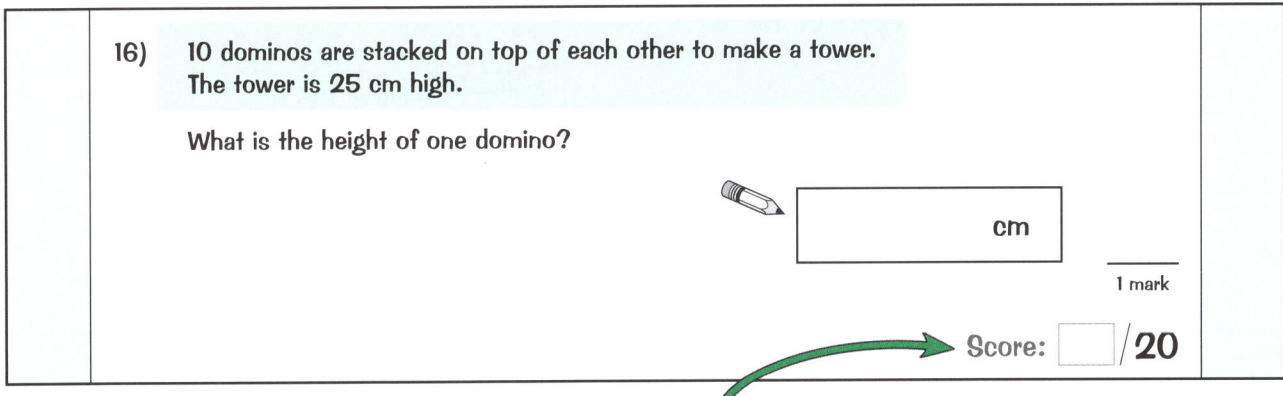

You can <u>add up your score</u> at the end to see how many you got right.

Use the Tick Boxes to Say How You're Doing

At the end of each topic, you'll see <u>faces</u> like the ones at the bottom of this page. <u>Tick</u> the one that matches how <u>confident</u> you feel with the <u>questions</u> on the page.

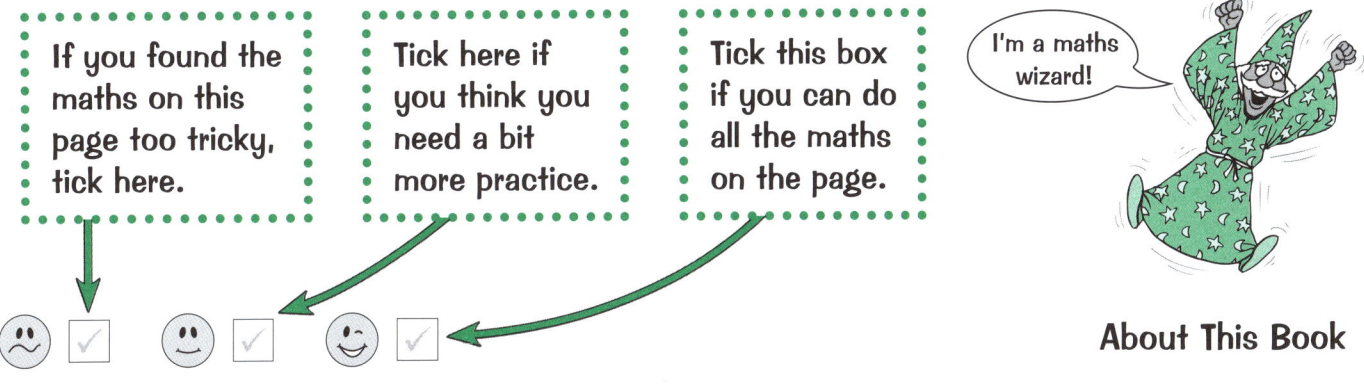

About This Book

Year Three Objectives Test

1) Count up in steps of 4 to fill in the boxes.

12 , 16 , ☐ , ☐

1 mark

2) What number is:

10 more than 412?

1 mark

100 less than 330?

1 mark

3) These tickets have numbers on them.

393   435   312

Which number has a 3 in the 'ones' place?
Write your answer in <u>words</u>.

1 mark

4) Use a ruler to measure the perimeter of this triangle.

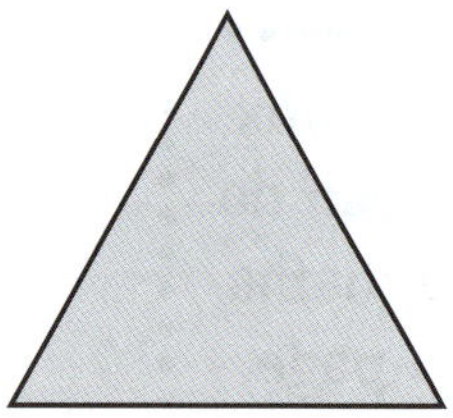

☐ cm

1 mark

Year Three Objectives Test

Year Three Objectives Test

5) Tick the two calculations below which are less than 30.

    12 × 2   5 × 8   9 × 3   8 × 4

☐   ☐   ☐   ☐

2 marks

6) Write down the number of faces on this shape.

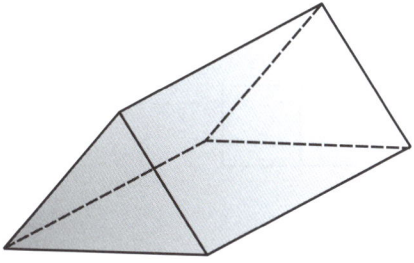

[____] faces

1 mark

7) Fill in the boxes to make these calculations correct.

712 + 50 = ☐

1 mark

205 − ☐ = 185

1 mark

8) Ashmita is making smoothies for her friends.

She needs these amounts of fruit:

| Lime 1 kg | Strawberry 950 g | Kiwi 1100 g |

Put the masses in order. Start with the heaviest.

☐ heaviest   ☐   ☐ lightest

1 mark

Year Three Objectives Test

9) Work out 127 + 344.

1 mark

10) Work out $\frac{2}{10} + \frac{3}{10}$.

Shade this shape to show your answer.

1 mark

11) The pictogram shows how many medals four friends have.

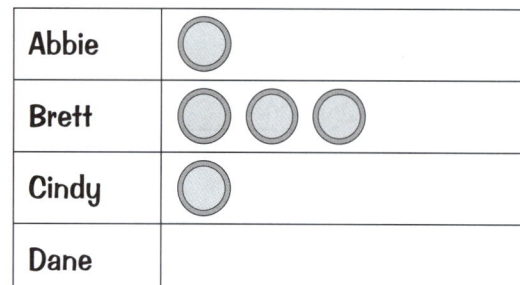

Key
◯ = 2 medals

How many medals do Abbie and Cindy have in total?

 medals

1 mark

Dane has 8 medals. Add this to the pictogram.

1 mark

12) Elsie draws a line on the grid below.

Use a ruler to draw a line that is perpendicular to Elsie's line.

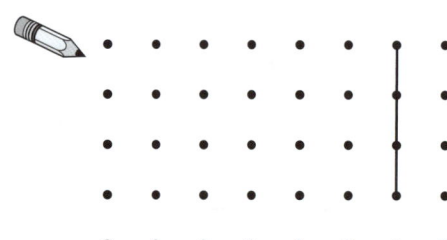

1 mark

Year Three Objectives Test

13) Dylan starts walking to the zoo at **8:50 am**.
He gets to the zoo at **9:30 am**.

How long did it take to walk to the zoo?

◯ minutes

1 mark

Dylan sees an ostrich and a giraffe at the zoo.

? m

2 m

The giraffe is three times as tall as the ostrich.
How tall is the giraffe? Give your answer in cm.

◯ cm

1 mark

14) There are **24 children** on a school playground.
A teacher divides the children into **3 equal groups**.

How many children are in each group?

◯ children

1 mark

There are three children wearing jumpers in each group.
How many children are not wearing jumpers in <u>total</u>?

◯ children

1 mark

Score: ◯ /20

Section One — Number and Place Value

Counting in Multiples

1) List the first four multiples of 6.

The first two have been done for you.

6 , 12 , ☐ , ☐

1 mark

2) List the first five multiples of 25.

Two have been done for you.

25 , ☐ , ☐ , 100 , ☐

1 mark

3) Starting at 2000, count forward two steps of 1000. What number do you reach?

☐

1 mark

4) List the first five multiples of 9.

One has been done for you.

☐ , 18 , ☐ , ☐ , ☐

1 mark

5) Circle the two numbers that are not multiples of 7.

14   25   7   35   37

1 mark

Counting Backwards Through Zero

1 Start at 0 and count back 6. Write down the number that you reach.

You can use this number line to help you.

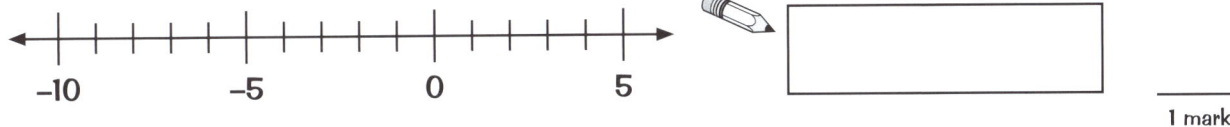

1 mark

2 Look at this number line.

Write the correct number in each box.

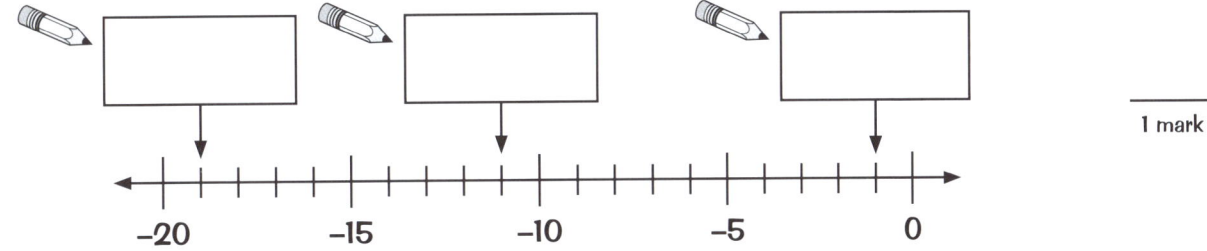

1 mark

3 Write 'less' or 'more' in the boxes to make these sentences correct.

2 marks

4 Start at 4 and count back three steps of 2. What number do you reach?

1 mark

5 How many steps of 1 are there between 5 and −3?

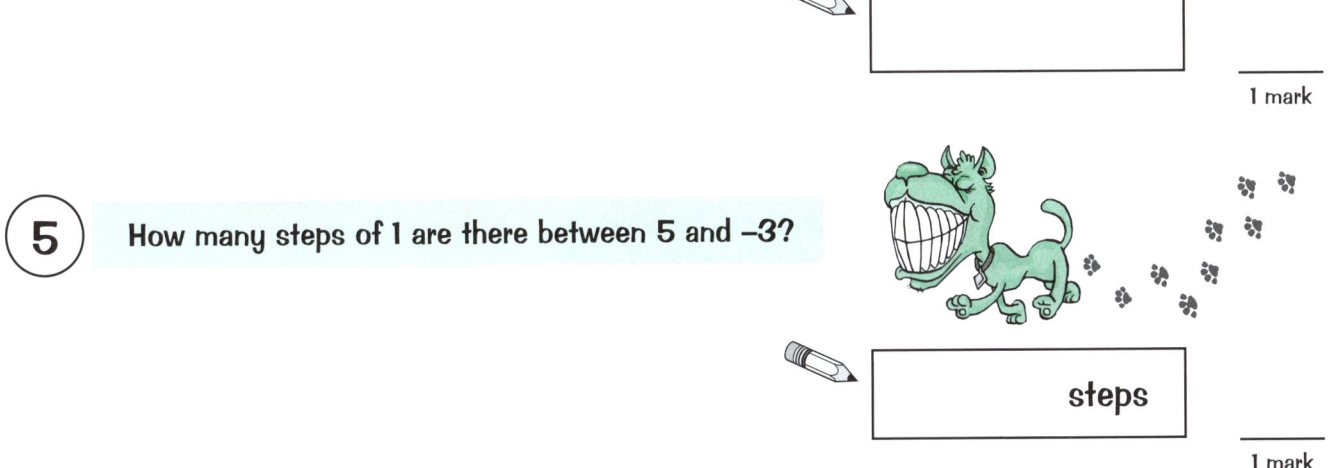

steps

1 mark

Section One — Number and Place Value

Place Value and Partitioning

1) Circle the number in the 'thousands' place in 1085.

0   1   5   8

1 mark

2) Match each number to the value of the underlined digit.

The first one has been done for you.

58<u>4</u>0 —————————————————\
<u>4</u>600 ————————— four ones\
5<u>4</u>35   four tens\
960<u>4</u>   four hundreds\
                                                  four thousands

1 mark

3) Partition 2456 into thousands, hundreds, tens and ones.

2456 = ☐ + ☐ + ☐ + ☐

1 mark

4) Write down the value of the 7 in 2700.

1 mark

5) What number do you get if you swap the digits in the 'ones' and 'thousands' place in 1066?

1 mark

Section One — Number and Place Value

1000 More or Less

1 Circle the number that is 1000 more than 3000.

    3100   2900   2000   4000

1 mark

2 Circle the number that is 1000 less than 9000.

    8900   9100   8000   9500

1 mark

3 Match each number to the number that is 1000 more than it.

The first one has been done for you.

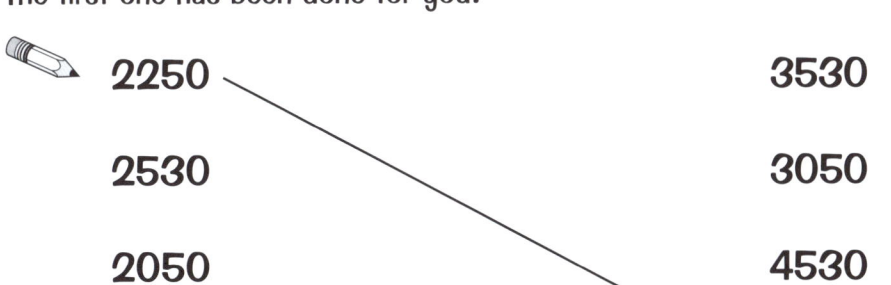

2250		3530
2530		3050
2050		4530
3530		3250

(2250 matched to 3250)

1 mark

4 Write down the number that is 1000 less than 5790.

1 mark

5 Circle the number that is 1000 less than 1154.

    2154   154   1054   115

1 mark

Section One — Number and Place Value

Ordering and Comparing Numbers

1 Circle the larger number in each pair.

8373   or   784   9500   or   4500

1 mark

2 Circle the smaller number in each pair.

5450   or   2007   4780   or   7480

1 mark

3 Write 'larger' or 'smaller' in the boxes to make these sentences correct.

4580 is [   ] than 580.

1 mark

7512 is [   ] than 6999.

1 mark

4 Put these numbers in order. Start with the largest.

7880   900   4303

[   ]   [   ]   [   ]
largest   smallest

1 mark

5 Look at these numbers.

Circle the largest number.

9840   4890   984   9485

1 mark

Section One — Number and Place Value

Ordering and Comparing Numbers

6 The page below shows how many hours four light bulbs have been on for.

Bulb A 8521
Bulb B 3584
Bulb C 989
Bulb D 1476

Which bulb has been on for the most time?

[ ]

1 mark

Which bulb has been on for the least time?

[ ]

1 mark

7 Put these numbers in order. Start with the smallest.

2450   2880   1450   1840

[ ] [ ] [ ] [ ]
smallest   largest

1 mark

8 Look at these numbers. Write > or < in each box.

4510 [ ] 8510   7492 [ ] 7415

2 marks

9 Write down a four-digit number larger than 9997.

[ ]

1 mark

Section One — Number and Place Value

Rounding

1) What is 11 rounded to the nearest 10?

Circle the correct answer.

20   10   0   15

1 mark

2) The numbers on the cards have been marked on this number line.

Round each number to the nearest 10.

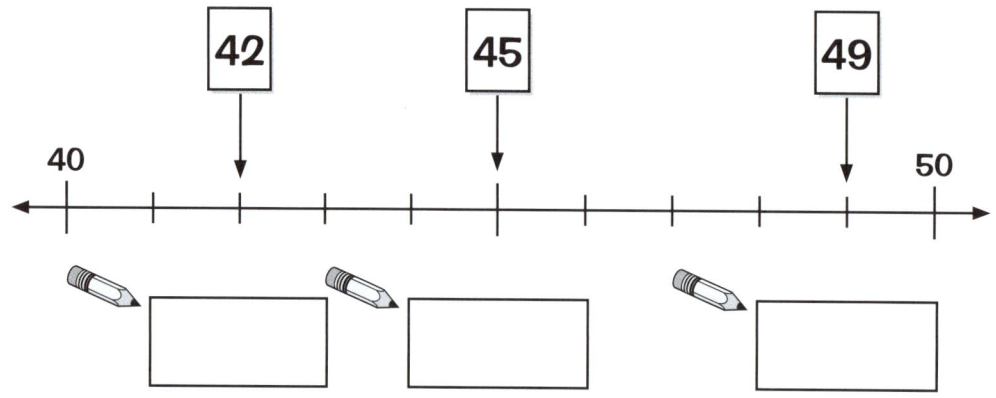

1 mark

3) Round these numbers to the nearest 1000.

Put a cross on the number line to show your answer.
The first one has been done for you.

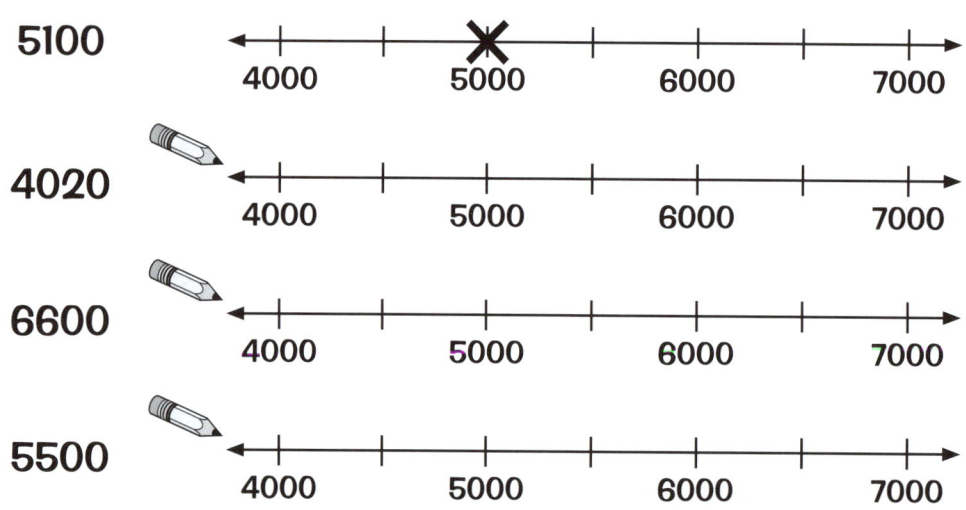

1 mark

4) Circle all the numbers that round to 70, to the nearest 10.

75   71   78   67   64

1 mark

Section One — Number and Place Value

Rounding

5 What is 512 rounded:

to the nearest 100?

to the nearest 10?

1 mark

6 Circle all the numbers that round to 200, to the nearest 100.

140   280   485   160   230

1 mark

7 Round 2419 to the nearest:

10   100   1000

1 mark

8 Match each number to the number it rounds to when rounded to the nearest 100.

One has been done for you.

5214 ———————————— 5200

5527   5300

5378   5400

5310   5500

5550   5600

2 marks

Section One — Number and Place Value

Decimal Numbers and Fractions

1 Write as a fraction:

one eighth

two sixths

2 marks

2 Shade $\frac{1}{3}$ of each of these shapes.

2 marks

3 Write as a decimal:

zero point one

three point eight

2 marks

4 Draw straight lines to match the descriptions to the decimals on the right.

5 tenths   0.05

5 hundredths   5.5

5 ones and 5 tenths   0.5

1 mark

Section One — Number and Place Value

Roman Numerals

1) Which Roman numeral shows the number 10?

Circle the correct answer.

   D   L   I   X

1 mark

2) Which number is shown by the Roman numeral C?

Circle the correct answer.

   2   5   50   100

1 mark

3) Match the Roman numerals to the numbers they represent.

One has been done for you.

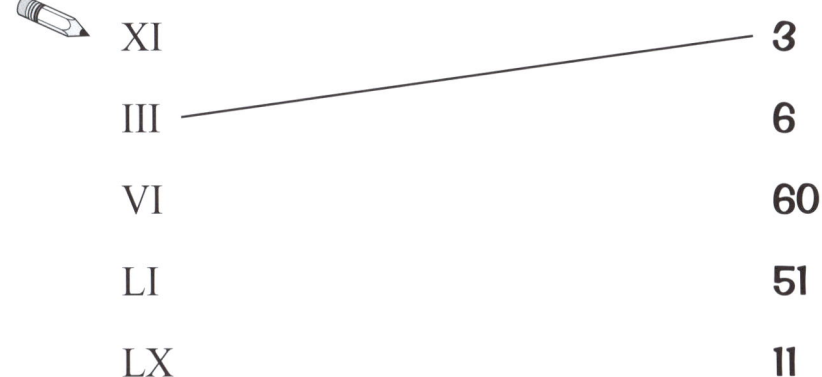

2 marks

4) Fill in the missing Roman numerals.

12 = X ☐ ☐

4 = ☐ V

24 = X ☐ I ☐

2 marks

Section One — Number and Place Value

Solving Number Problems

1 A helicopter starts at a height of 2500 m. It drops 1000 m.

What height is the helicopter at now?

[_____] m

1 mark

2 A squirrel collects 25 nuts each day.

Count up in steps of 25 to find how many nuts the squirrel collects in three days.

[_____] nuts

1 mark

Round the number of nuts collected <u>each day</u> to the nearest 10.

[_____] nuts

1 mark

3 Three knights have finished a contest.
The number of points they each got is shown below.

Round each of the numbers to the nearest 100.

Percy	4287
Arthur	1455
Flo	7120

[_____]

[_____]

[_____]

1 mark

Who got the most points?

[_____]

1 mark

Section One — Number and Place Value

Solving Number Problems

4 Meera is at a train station. A train goes past her every 6 minutes.

How many trains go past her in 18 minutes?

trains

1 mark

Meera gets on a train with six carriages. Five of the carriages are full.

What fraction of the carriages are full?

1 mark

5 Look at these Roman numerals. Write > or < in each box.

III ☐ X   L ☐ VI

1 mark

6 A lighthouse is 25 m tall. The sea floor is 10 m below the surface of the sea.

How many metres are there between the top of the lighthouse and the sea floor?

metres

1 mark

Section One — Number and Place Value

Section Two — Calculations

Written Addition

1 Work out:

```
  5 4 6
+ 4 0 1
───────
```

```
  4 2 4 3
+ 2 0 4 5
─────────
```

2 marks

2 Calculate 2247 + 5211.

1 mark

3 Work out these sums.

4578 + 4721

1 mark

3513 + 429

1 mark

4 What is the answer to 950 + 348?

1 mark

Written Subtraction

1 Calculate:

```
   5 8 7
 - 1 5 2
```

```
   5 7 7 9
 - 3 3 6 5
```

2 marks

2 Work out 756 − 245.

1 mark

3 Work out:

4285 − 2712

1 mark

6466 − 2159

1 mark

4 Use a written method to work out 8984 − 568.

1 mark

Section Two — Calculations

Estimating and Checking

1 Which of these is an inverse calculation for 54 + 12 = 66?

Circle the correct answer.

54 − 12 = 66   66 − 12 = 54

12 + 66 = 54   54 − 66 = 12

1 mark

2 Waldo wants to work out the answer to 142 + 79.

Fill in the boxes using numbers from the cloud.

Cloud contains: 150, 80, 200, 70, 140, 60

142 is about ☐.

79 is about ☐.

1 mark

Use your answers above to write down an estimate to 142 + 79.

☐

1 mark

3 Minnie works out 132 − 37 = 95.

Fill in the boxes to make an inverse calculation to check she's right.

☐ = ☐ + ☐

1 mark

4 Circle the best estimate of the answer to 201 + 498.

800   700   600   300

1 mark

Section Two — Calculations

Estimating and Checking

5) Here are three calculations.

Write down the answers to the inverse calculations.

13 × 5 = 65   65 ÷ 13 =

84 ÷ 4 = 21   21 × 4 =

12 × 6 = 72   72 ÷ 12 =

2 marks

6) Circle the best estimate for the answer to 52 × 5.

450   250   500   100

1 mark

7) Robbie needs to give his plant 2 g of plant food each week for 19 weeks. He estimates that he will need about 90 g of plant food in total.

Explain why Robbie is wrong and give a better estimate.

2 marks

Section Two — Calculations

Using Times Tables

1) Work out:

3 × 6 = ☐   9 × 6 = ☐

2 marks

2) Calculate:

2 × 11 = ☐   8 × 11 = ☐

2 marks

3) Circle all the numbers that are in the 9 times table.

45   18   49   12   90

1 mark

4) Use the 7 times tables to fill in these boxes.

☐ × 7 = 21   63 ÷ 7 = ☐

2 marks

5) Cans of cola come in packs of 12. Colin buys 4 packs.

How many <u>cans</u> of cola does Colin buy?

☐ cans

1 mark

Section Two — Calculations

Mental Multiplying and Dividing

This page is on <u>mental</u> maths, so you need to do these calculations in your head.

1 Fill in the boxes to make these calculations correct.

5 × 7 = ☐   5 × 70 = ☐

2 marks

2 Calculate:

4 × 11 = ☐

1 mark

4 × 11 × 2 = ☐

1 mark

3 Circle all the calculations below that have 0 as the answer.

95 × 0   3 × 1   0 × 4   1 × 1   2 × 3

1 mark

4 Fill in the boxes to complete these calculations.

53 × 1 = ☐   17 ÷ 1 = ☐

2 marks

5 Myrtle has 60 flowers.

She gives an equal number of flowers to each of her 12 friends. How many flowers does each friend get?

☐ flowers

1 mark

Section Two — Calculations

Factor Pairs

1 Find the missing values.

3 × ☐ = 12   2 × ☐ = 12

1 mark

2 All the factors of 18 are shown below.

Draw lines to join up the factor pairs of 18.

6

1   9

2   3

18

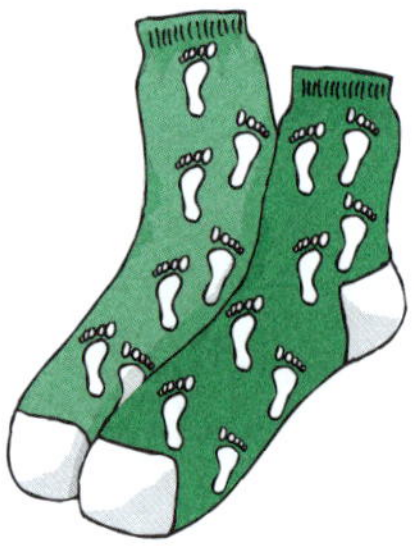

1 mark

3 List all the factor pairs of 4.

1 mark

4 Circle the pair that is not a factor pair of 16.

1 and 16   4 and 4   8 and 2   10 and 6

1 mark

5 Fill in the boxes to make this calculation correct.

☐ × ☐ = 3

1 mark

Written Multiplication

1) Use a written method to work out these multiplications.

Show your working.

42 × 4

14 × 7

2 marks

2) Calculate:

213 × 3

126 × 7

2 marks

3) What is 341 lots of 9?

Show your working.

2 marks

Section Two — Calculations

Solving Calculation Problems

1) 1325 cars crossed a bridge on Sunday and 7512 cars crossed the bridge on Monday.

Work out how many cars crossed the bridge in total.

[_____ cars]

1 mark

2) Frankie scores 12 points in a quiz. Percy scores six times as many points.

How many points did Percy score?

[_____ points]

1 mark

How many points did Frankie and Percy score altogether?

[_____ points]

1 mark

3) A story book has 1449 pages. A textbook has 374 pages.

How many more pages are in the story book than in the textbook?

[_____ pages]

1 mark

How many pages do the two books have in total?

[_____ pages]

1 mark

Section Two — Calculations

Solving Calculation Problems

4 Llewelyn reads 4 gardening magazines and 3 history magazines each week.

What is the total number of magazines he reads in 7 weeks?

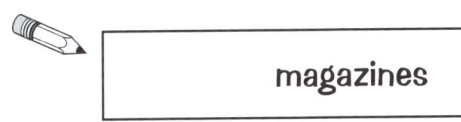
magazines

1 mark

5 Jean goes to the swimming pool twice a day.
On each visit, she swims 8 laps.

How many laps does she swim each day?

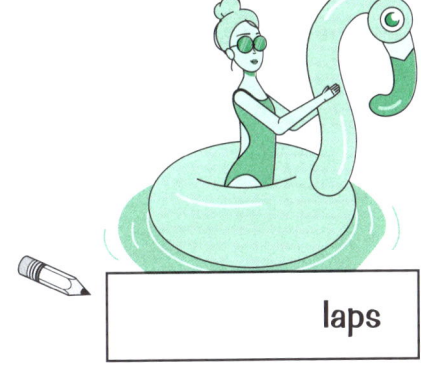
laps

1 mark

How many laps does she swim in eight days?
Show your working.

laps

2 marks

6 There are two slides and five swings at each park in Vincente's city.
In total, there are 18 slides.

How many parks are there in the city?

parks

1 mark

How many swings are there in the city?

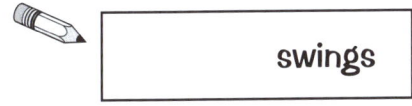
swings

1 mark

Section Three — Fractions and Decimals

Counting in Hundredths

1) Count forward in hundredths to fill in the boxes.

$\frac{51}{100}$, $\frac{52}{100}$, $\frac{\square}{100}$, $\frac{\square}{100}$

1 mark

2) Draw lines to match each fraction with the correct words.

$\frac{95}{100}$ $\frac{2}{100}$ $\frac{20}{100}$

twenty hundredths   ninety five hundredths   two hundredths

1 mark

3) The shape below is divided into 100 equal parts.

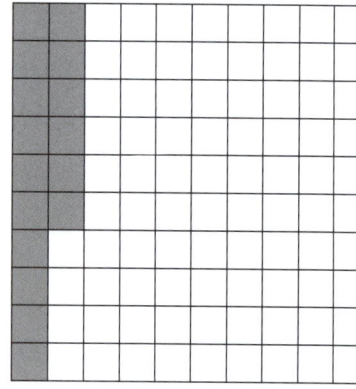

How many hundredths are shaded?

☐ hundredths

1 mark

Another three hundredths are shaded.
How many hundredths are now shaded?

☐ hundredths

1 mark

4) One tenth of this shape is shaded.

If each tenth is divided into 10 equal parts, how many hundredths of the shape will be shaded?

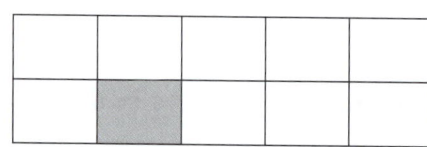

☐ hundredths

1 mark

Section Three — Fractions and Decimals

Equivalent Fractions

1 Look at the shaded shape.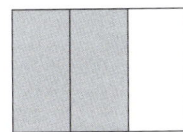

Tick the shape which has the same fraction shaded as the shape above.

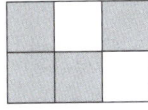 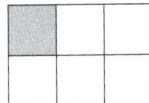 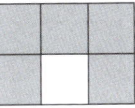

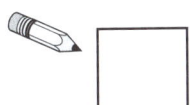

1 mark

2 The shape below has $\frac{8}{20}$ shaded.

Shade the shapes on the right so they have the same fraction shaded as the shape on the left.

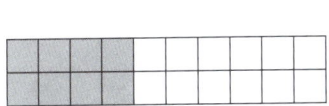 =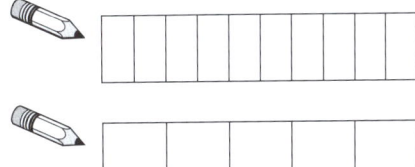

1 mark

3 These two shapes each have a fraction shaded.

How many more parts would you need to shade on shape B to make the shapes show equivalent fractions?

A 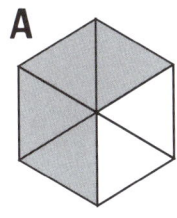 B 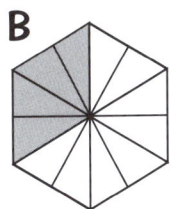   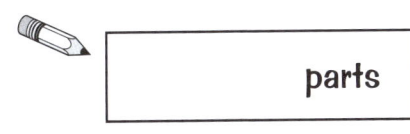 parts

1 mark

4 Circle **two** fractions below that are equivalent to $\frac{1}{2}$.

$\frac{4}{8}$ $\frac{3}{4}$ $\frac{5}{10}$ $\frac{1}{6}$

2 marks

Section Three — Fractions and Decimals

Adding and Subtracting Fractions

1 Shade in the final shape to show the answer.

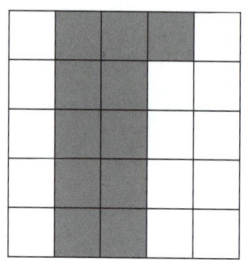 +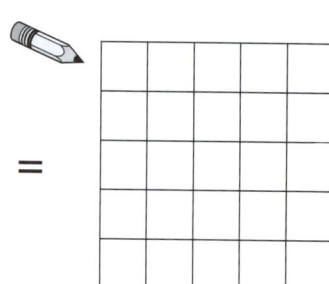

1 mark

2 Calculate:

$\frac{1}{8} + \frac{4}{8} = \frac{\square}{8}$

$\frac{6}{10} + \frac{3}{10} = \frac{\square}{10}$

2 marks

3 $\frac{6}{16}$ of the shape below has been shaded.

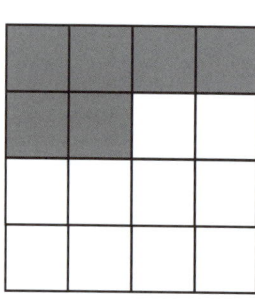

Shade in another $\frac{8}{16}$.

1 mark

What fraction of the shape is now shaded?

1 mark

4 What is two sixths plus three sixths?

Write your answer as a fraction.

1 mark

Section Three — Fractions and Decimals

Adding and Subtracting Fractions

5) Natalie has a doughnut. She eats $\frac{2}{5}$ of it.

What fraction of her doughnut is left? You can shade in the diagram to help.

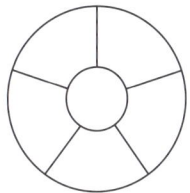

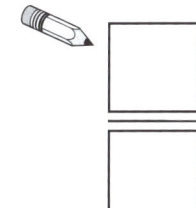

1 mark

6) What is $\frac{4}{9} + \frac{7}{9}$?

Circle the correct answer.

$\frac{1}{9}$ $\frac{11}{9}$ $\frac{13}{9}$ $\frac{9}{4}$

1 mark

7) Fill in the missing numbers.

$\frac{4}{5} - \frac{\square}{5} = \frac{3}{5}$ $1 - \frac{\square}{6} = \frac{4}{6}$

2 marks

8) The hives below are made up of 7 hexagons each.

What is the total fraction shaded?

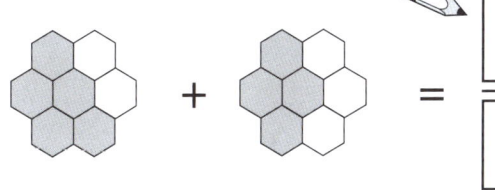

$= \frac{\square}{\square}$

1 mark

Section Three — Fractions and Decimals

Fractions of Amounts

1 Circle $\frac{2}{3}$ of the biscuits below.

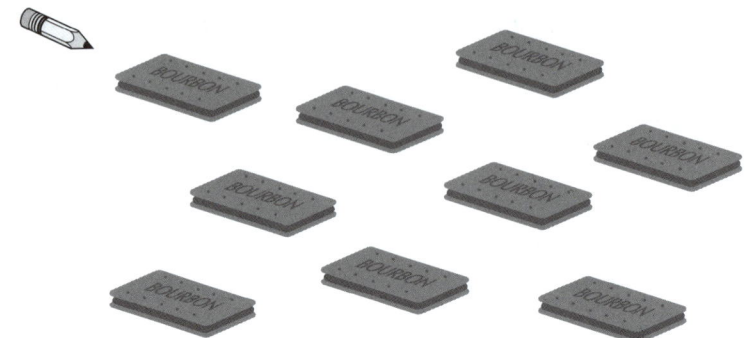

1 mark

2 This robot head is made up of ten equal squares. Shade in $\frac{4}{5}$ of its head.

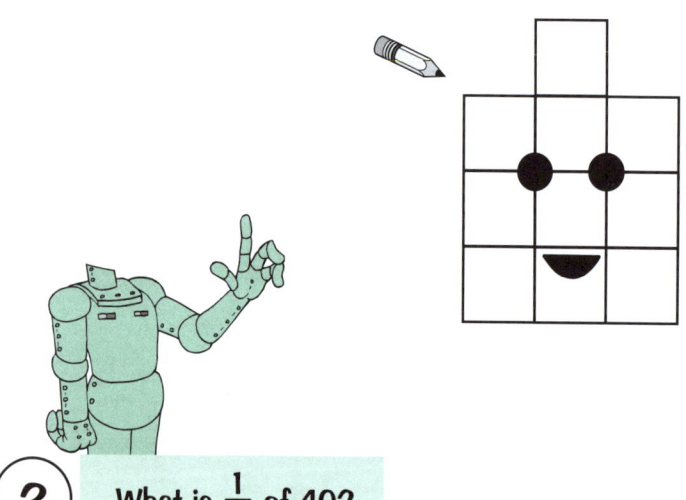

1 mark

3 What is $\frac{1}{5}$ of 40?

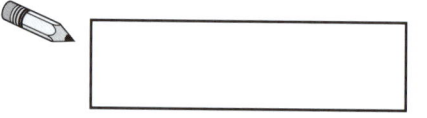

1 mark

4 What is $\frac{2}{6}$ of 30? Circle the correct answer.

   5   10   12   20

1 mark

Section Three — Fractions and Decimals

Fractions of Amounts

5 Fill in the boxes to complete the sentences.

$\frac{1}{4}$ of 16 is ☐ , so $\frac{3}{4}$ of 16 is ☐ .

1 mark

$\frac{1}{10}$ of 50 is ☐ , so $\frac{7}{10}$ of 50 is ☐ .

1 mark

6 What is four tenths of 100?

☐

1 mark

7 There are 27 prizes to be won at a fairground game.

$\frac{2}{3}$ of the prizes are teddy bears. How many teddy bears are there?

☐ teddy bears

1 mark

8 Ameena likes $\frac{1}{5}$ of the songs on her sister's playlist.

There are 35 songs on the playlist. How many songs does Ameena <u>not</u> like?

☐ songs

1 mark

Section Three — Fractions and Decimals

Decimals

1 What is the value of the 5 in each number? Circle the correct answer.

0.5   5 tenths / 5 hundredths

0.35   5 tenths / 5 hundredths

2 Here is a number line. Fill in the boxes with the missing numbers.

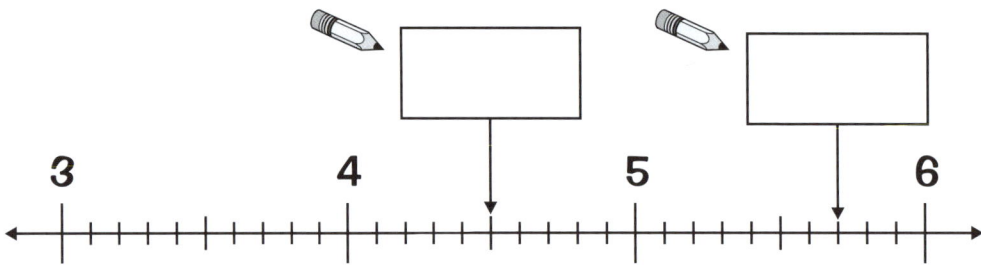

3 What number is equal to two tenths and one hundredth?

Circle the correct answer.

21   0.21   2.1   1.2

4 Fill in the boxes.

4 + 0.6 = ☐

7 + 0.3 + 0.08 = ☐

Section Three — Fractions and Decimals

Writing Fractions as Decimals

1 Draw lines to match the fraction with the decimal of the same value.

$\frac{90}{100}$ 0.6

$\frac{12}{100}$ 0.9

$\frac{6}{10}$ 0.44

$\frac{44}{100}$ 0.12

2 marks

2 What is $\frac{8}{100}$ as a decimal?

1 mark

3 What is $\frac{1}{4}$ as a decimal?

Circle the correct answer.

0.04   0.25   0.4   0.2

1 mark

4 Write the fraction that has been shaded on each shape as a decimal.

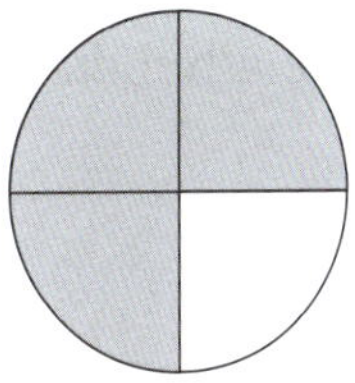

2 marks

Section Three — Fractions and Decimals

Dividing by 10 and 100

1 Work out:

50 ÷ 10 ☐   68 ÷ 10 ☐

1 mark

37 ÷ 10 ☐   9 ÷ 10 ☐

1 mark

2 What is 81 divided by 10? Circle the correct answer.

810   0.81   1.8   8.1

1 mark

3 What is 26 divided by 100? Circle the correct answer.

2.6   260   0.26   0.026

1 mark

4 What number is one hundred times smaller than 93?

☐

1 mark

Section Three — Fractions and Decimals

Dividing by 10 and 100

5 40 pieces of fruit are shared between 10 people.

How many pieces of fruit does each person get?

_____ pieces

1 mark

6 A jumbo-sized cake weighs 32 kg. The cake is cut into 100 equal slices.

How much does each slice weigh?

_____ kg

1 mark

7 Calculate the following and mark the answers with an arrow on the number line.

20 ÷ 100   17 ÷ 10   9 ÷ 10

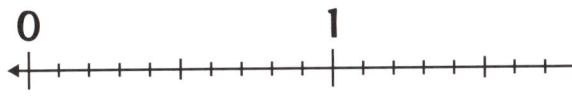

2 marks

8 Freya divides a number by 10. Her new number is 0.8.

What number did she start with? Circle the correct answer.

8   0.8   80   0.08

1 mark

Section Three — Fractions and Decimals

Rounding Decimals

1 Round each number shown on the number line to the nearest whole number.

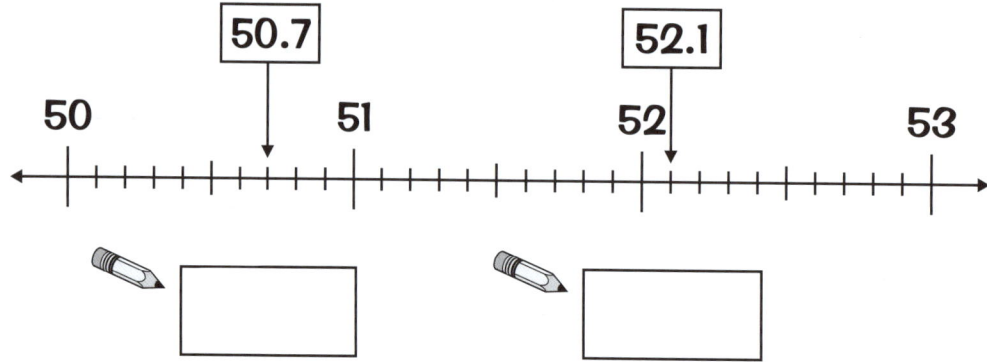

2 marks

2 Round each number to the nearest whole number.

6.7 ☐   14.9 ☐

9.3 ☐   30.5 ☐

2 marks

3 Gwen throws a ball 4.2 m. Round this to the nearest whole metre.

Circle the correct answer.

4.2 m   5 m   4.5 m   4 m

1 mark

4 What is 99.8 rounded to the nearest whole number?

☐

1 mark

Section Three — Fractions and Decimals

Comparing Decimals

1 Which number is bigger? Circle the correct answer.

22.4   23.7

1 mark

2 Write the numbers in order. Start with the smallest.

6.5   7.2   6.1

smallest   largest

1 mark

3 The numbers below are in order from smallest to largest.

Which position would 9.13 go in? Write down the correct letter.

       A   B   C

8.60 ↓ 8.88 ↓ 9.45 ↓

1 mark

4 Four friends buy some food from a fish 'n' chips shop. They each spend a different amount of money.

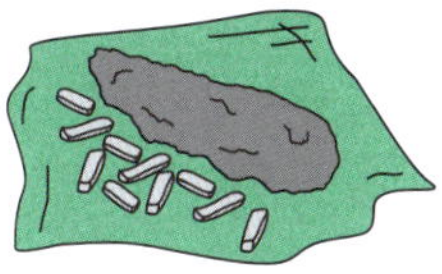

Write the amounts in order. Start with the least amount spent.

£3.15   £3.50   £2.85   £3.35

least spent   most spent

1 mark

Section Three — Fractions and Decimals

Solving Fraction and Decimal Problems

1 A band of pirates find some treasure.

They spend $\frac{1}{8}$ of it on eye patches and $\frac{5}{8}$ of it on parrots.

What fraction of their treasure did they spend?

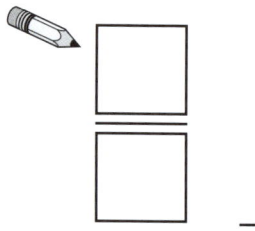

1 mark

2 Mariko pays £46 for 10 rock climbing lessons.

How much does one lesson cost?
Circle the correct answer.

 £0.46   £460   £4.60

1 mark

3 Gavin has a tin of paint and uses $\frac{5}{6}$ of it to paint a wall.

What fraction of paint does he have left?

$\frac{\Box}{6}$

1 mark

4 Mei has 12 pets. 6 of her pets are chickens.

Circle <u>three</u> fractions that give the fraction of Mei's pets that are chickens.

   $\frac{2}{4}$ $\frac{1}{2}$ $\frac{1}{12}$ $\frac{2}{6}$ $\frac{6}{12}$

2 marks

Section Three — Fractions and Decimals

Solving Fraction and Decimal Problems

5 Celia is given four presents for her birthday. Their weights are given below.

| 0.35 kg | 1.2 kg | 0.12 kg | 1.3 kg |
| A | B | C | D |

Which present is the heaviest?

1 mark

Which present weighs 10 times less than present B?

1 mark

6 Oskar jumps 3.8 metres in the long jump.

On his second jump he jumps 0.4 metres more.
Count forwards in steps of 0.1 m to work out how far his second jump was.

_____ m

1 mark

Round the first jump to the nearest whole metre.

_____ m

1 mark

7 Anna-Maria saved £24.

She spends $\frac{3}{4}$ of it on books.
How much money does she have left?

£ _____

1 mark

Section Three — Fractions and Decimals

Section Four — Measurement

Units

1 Convert these measurements:

2 kg to g ⟶ ☐ g

4 litres to ml ⟶ ☐ ml

2 marks

2 Write the correct length in each box.

Give your answers in mm.

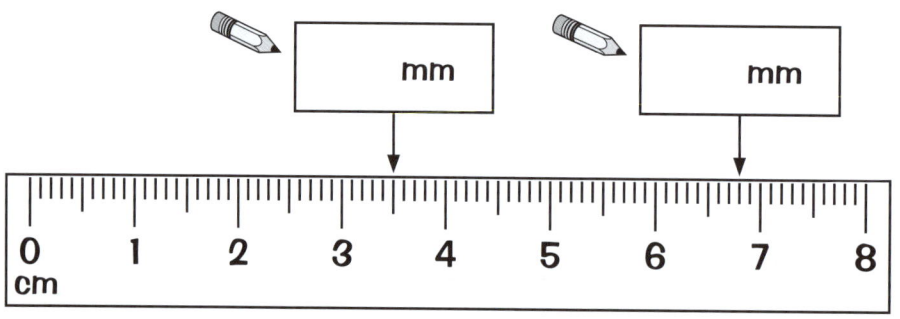

1 mark

3 Reuben runs a marathon in 3 hours.

How many minutes is this? Circle the correct answer.

90   180   300   120

1 mark

4 Match up each length on the left to the same length on the right.

The first one has been done for you.

5 m ⟶ 500 cm
5 km — 50 cm
0.5 km — 5000 m
0.5 m — 500 m

2 marks

Section Four — Measurement

Units

5 Three friends measure their heights.

Enzo
1.3 m

Tonya
125 cm

Luce
135 cm

Who is the shortest?

1 mark

6 Faiza has a bucket with 8 litres of milk in it.
She adds 0.5 litres of milk.

How much milk is now in the bucket?
Write your answer in ml.

 ml

1 mark

7 Parcel A weighs 1.2 kg.
Parcel B is weighed on these scales.

How much heavier is Parcel B than Parcel A?

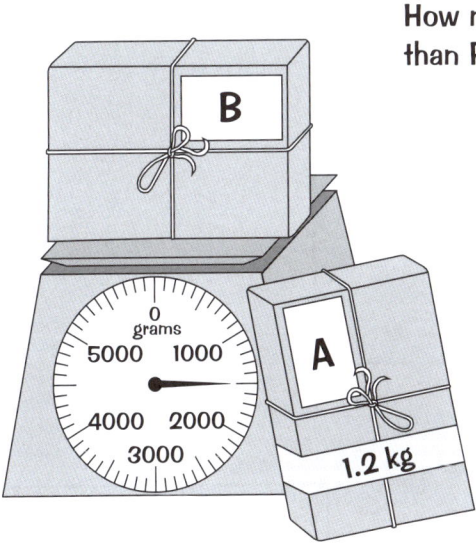
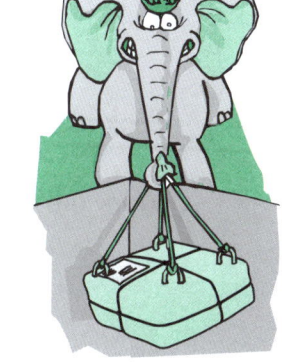

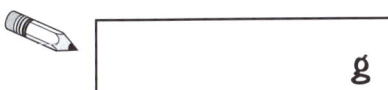 g

1 mark

Section Four — Measurement

Perimeter

1) Work out the perimeter of each square.

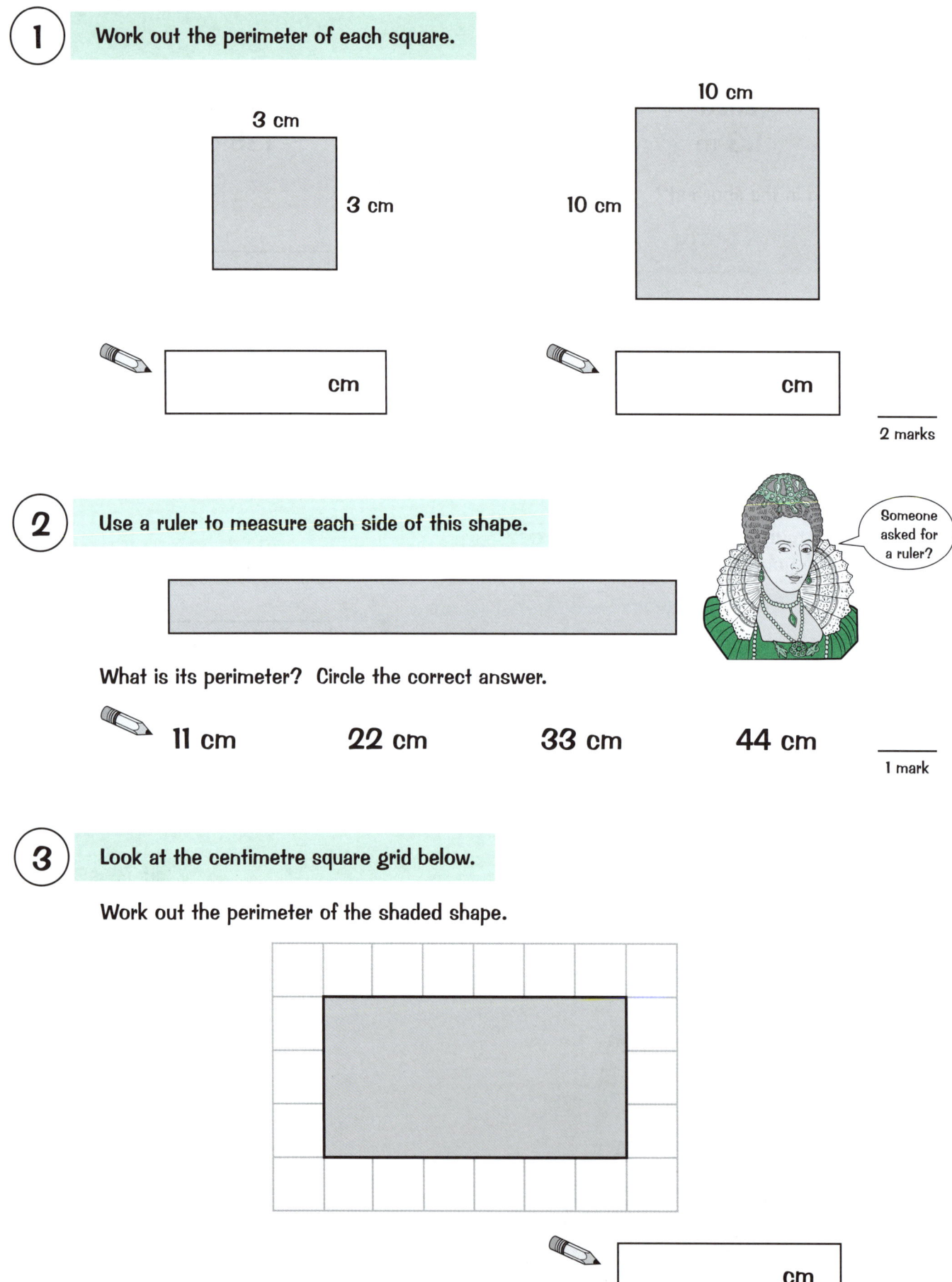

2 marks

2) Use a ruler to measure each side of this shape.

What is its perimeter? Circle the correct answer.

11 cm   22 cm   33 cm   44 cm

1 mark

3) Look at the centimetre square grid below.

Work out the perimeter of the shaded shape.

1 mark

Perimeter

4 Calculate the perimeter of this notice board.

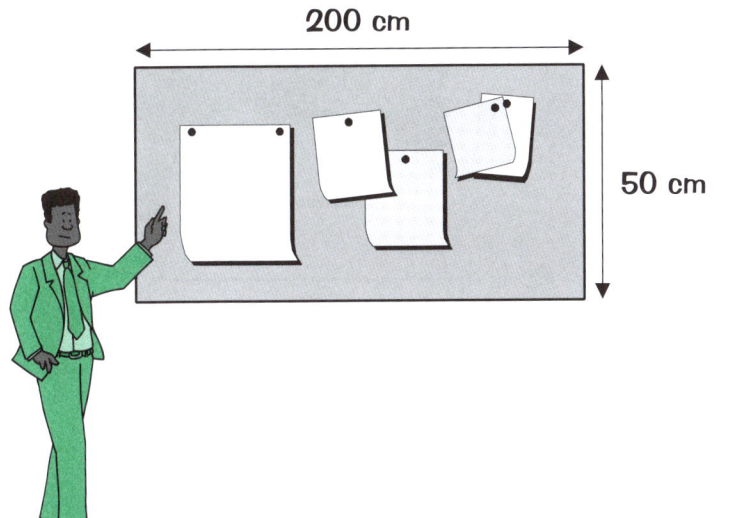

 cm

1 mark

5 A square room has a perimeter of 16 m.

How long is one side of the room? Circle the correct answer.

 2 m   64 m   4 m   16 m

1 mark

6 Two shapes are shown below.

How much longer is the perimeter of Shape B than Shape A?
Show your working.

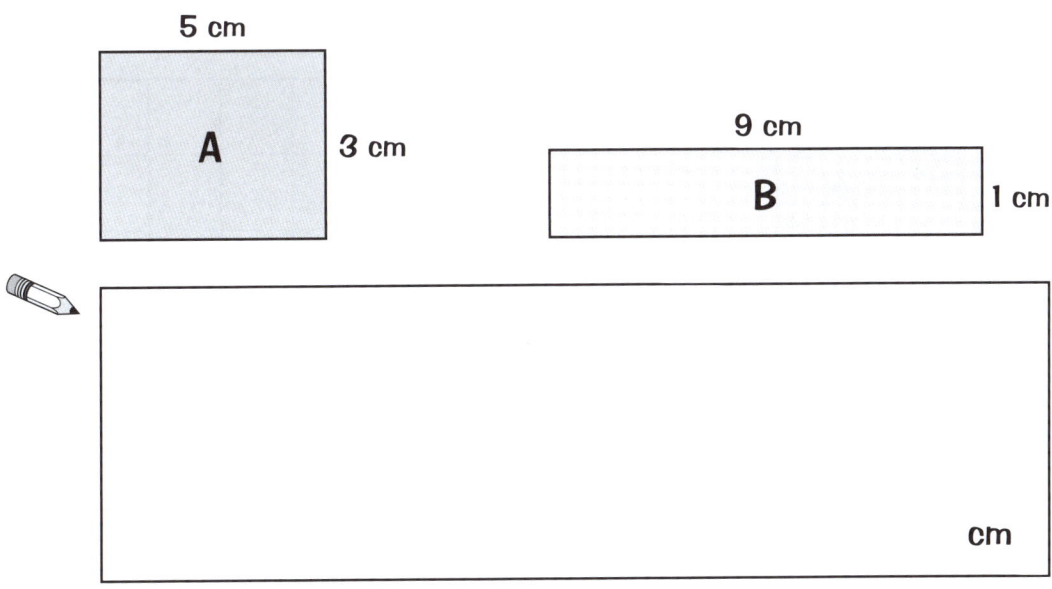

cm

2 marks

Section Four — Measurement

Area

1 Look at the grid below.

How many squares make up the shaded shape?

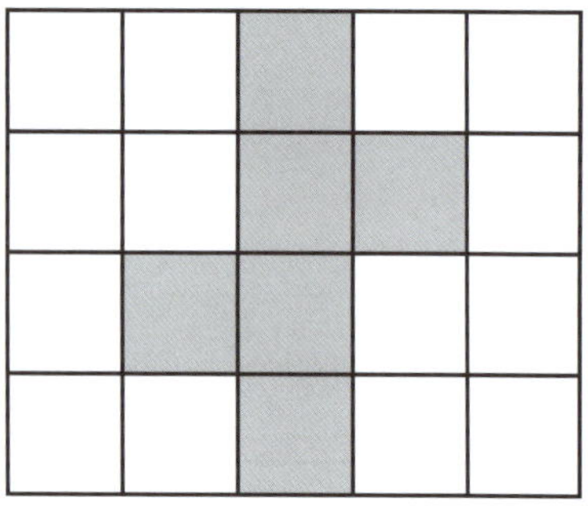

[ ] squares

1 mark

2 The grids below are made up of square centimetres.

Find the area of each shaded shape.

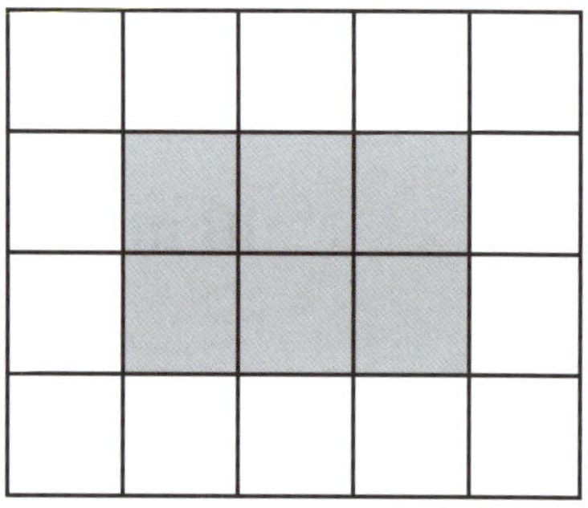

[ ] cm²

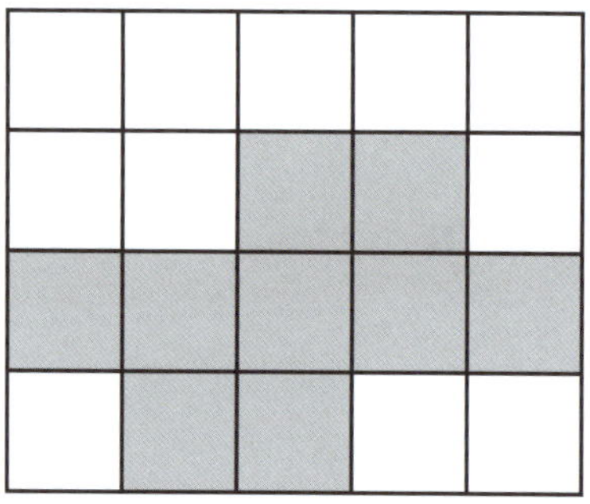

[ ] cm²

[ ] cm²

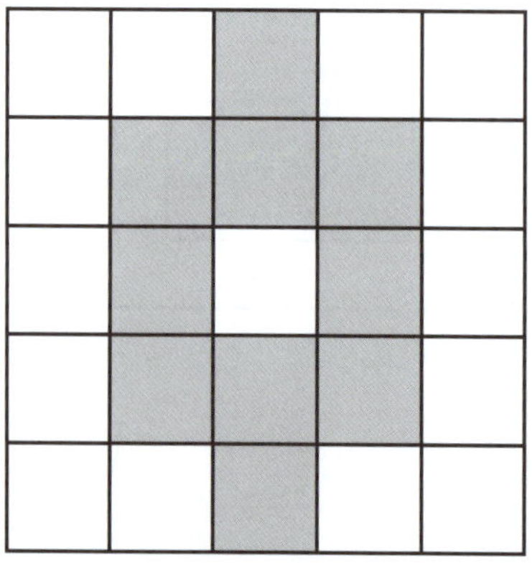

[ ] cm²

2 marks

Section Four — Measurement

Area

3 Roopesh has a grid made up of centimetre squares.
He shades some squares to make three different shapes.

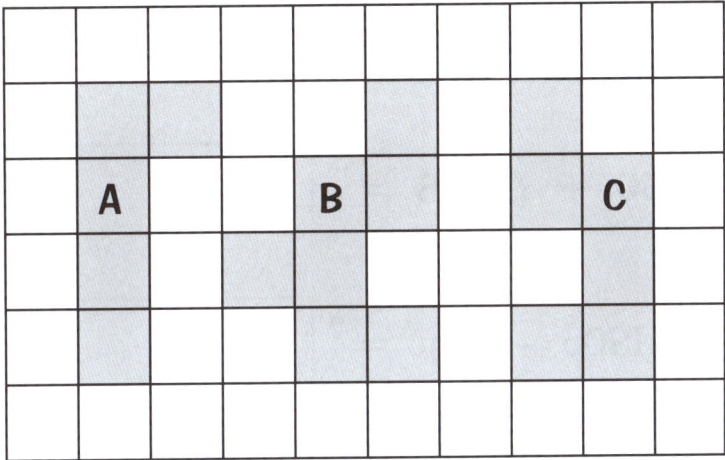

Which shape has the largest area? Circle the correct answer.

    Shape A   Shape B   Shape C

1 mark

Which shape has an area of 6 cm²? Circle the correct answer.

    Shape A   Shape B   Shape C

1 mark

4 On the grid below, each square has an area of 1 cm².

Shade more squares to make a shape with an area of 14 cm².

 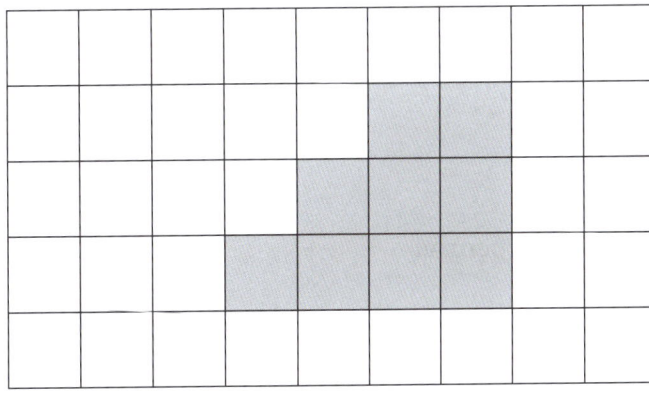

1 mark

Section Four — Measurement

Money

1 Work out these calculations.
Give your answers in pounds (£).

80p + 40p = £ ☐

£1.50 + £0.55 = £ ☐

130p − 60p = £ ☐

£2.20 − 20p − 10p = £ ☐

2 A watermelon costs £2.10.
A pumpkin costs twice as much.

How much does a pumpkin cost?

£ ☐

3 Carina has £3.12. She loses a 50 pence coin on the bus.

How much money does she have now?

£ ☐

4 £1.80 is shared between 3 people.

How much does each person get? Circle the correct answer.

£0.60   50p   30p   £0.10

Section Four — Measurement

Money

5 Paul sees some animal playing cards in a shop.

Circle the card which costs the least amount of money.

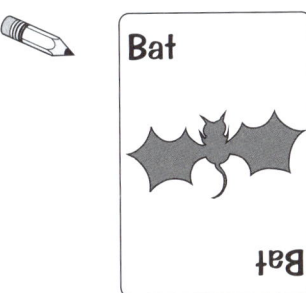  

£0.22 21p £0.19

1 mark

He buys the 'Cat' card and the 'Rat' card and pays with a £1 coin.

How much change does he get?

£ ____

1 mark

6 These piggy banks have different amounts of money in.

A B
£1.80 £1.15

Maya adds £1.50 to piggy bank A and £2.00 to piggy bank B.

Which piggy bank has more money? Show your working.

2 marks

Section Four — Measurement

Clocks

1 What time is shown on this clock? Put a tick in the correct box.

☐ twenty-two minutes past eleven

☐ four minutes past eleven

☐ eleven minutes past five

1 mark

2 Write in 12-hour clock format:

14:30 → ☐ : ☐ pm

20:45 → ☐ : ☐ pm

2 marks

3 Draw lines to match each clock to the correct digital time.

am   pm   am

02:05   02:40   17:55

2 marks

4 The clock below shows a time in the afternoon.

Write this time in 24-hour clock format.

☐ : ☐

1 mark

Section Four — Measurement

Time Problems

1 A singing contest is on for **3 weeks**.

Complete the sentence to find how many days the contest lasts.

1 week = ☐ days, so 3 weeks = 3 × ☐ = ☐ days

1 mark

2 Barney the budgie is 1 year and 6 months old.

How old is Barney in months?

☐ months

1 mark

3 Sam's birthday party is in the evening.
Here are the start and finish times for his party.

Start   Finish

How long is his party? Give your answer in minutes.

☐ minutes

1 mark

4 Kimiya runs twice around her school field.

She takes 3 minutes and 5 seconds to do the first lap.
She takes 200 seconds to do the second lap.

How many seconds does she run for in total?

☐ seconds

1 mark

Section Four — Measurement

Section Five — Geometry

Comparing 2D Shapes

1 Draw lines to match each quadrilateral with its name. One has been done for you.

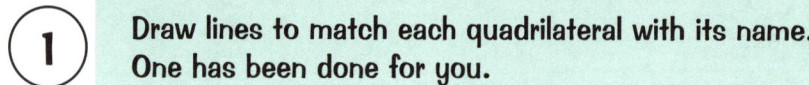

trapezium   rectangle   rhombus   kite

2 marks

2 Draw two more lines on the grid to make a right-angled triangle.

Use a ruler.

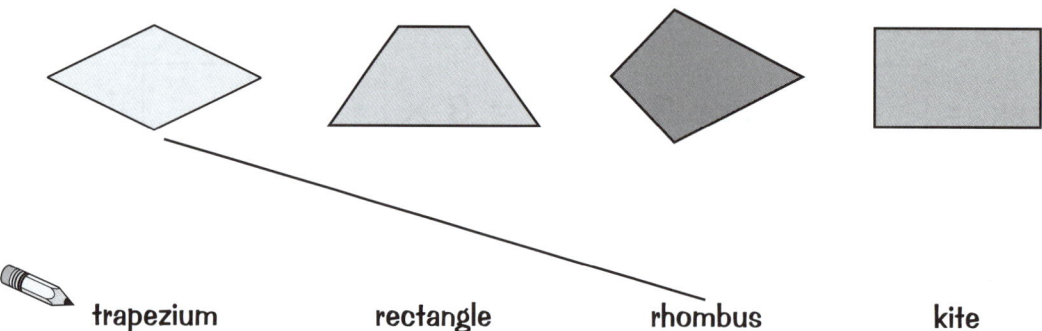

1 mark

3 Circle all the pentagons in this set of shapes.

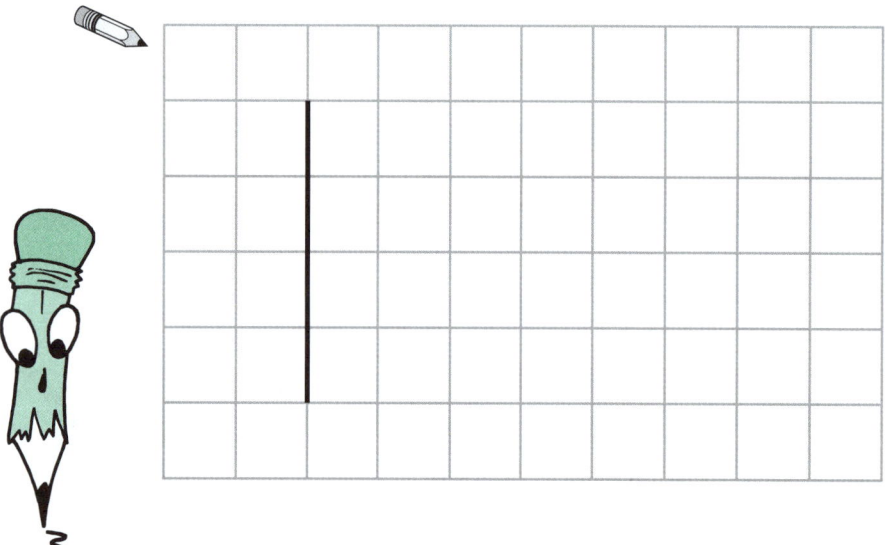

1 mark

Comparing 2D Shapes

4 Look at the triangles below.

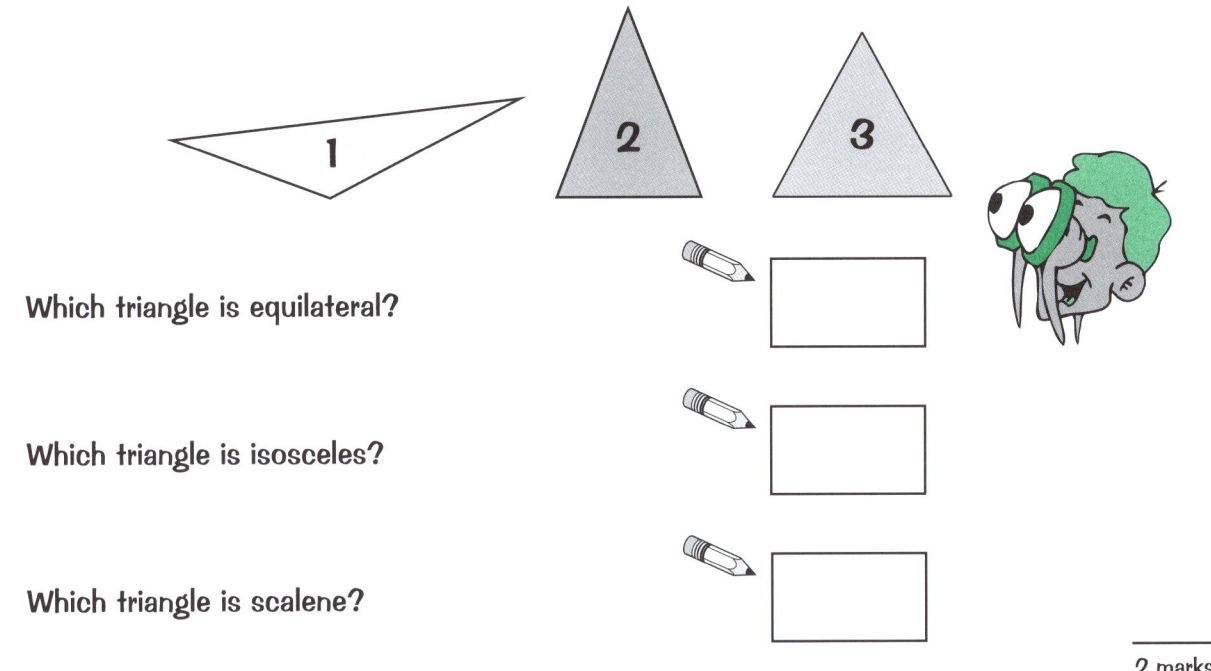

Which triangle is equilateral?

Which triangle is isosceles?

Which triangle is scalene?

2 marks

5 Fill in the boxes to make the sentences about this shape correct.

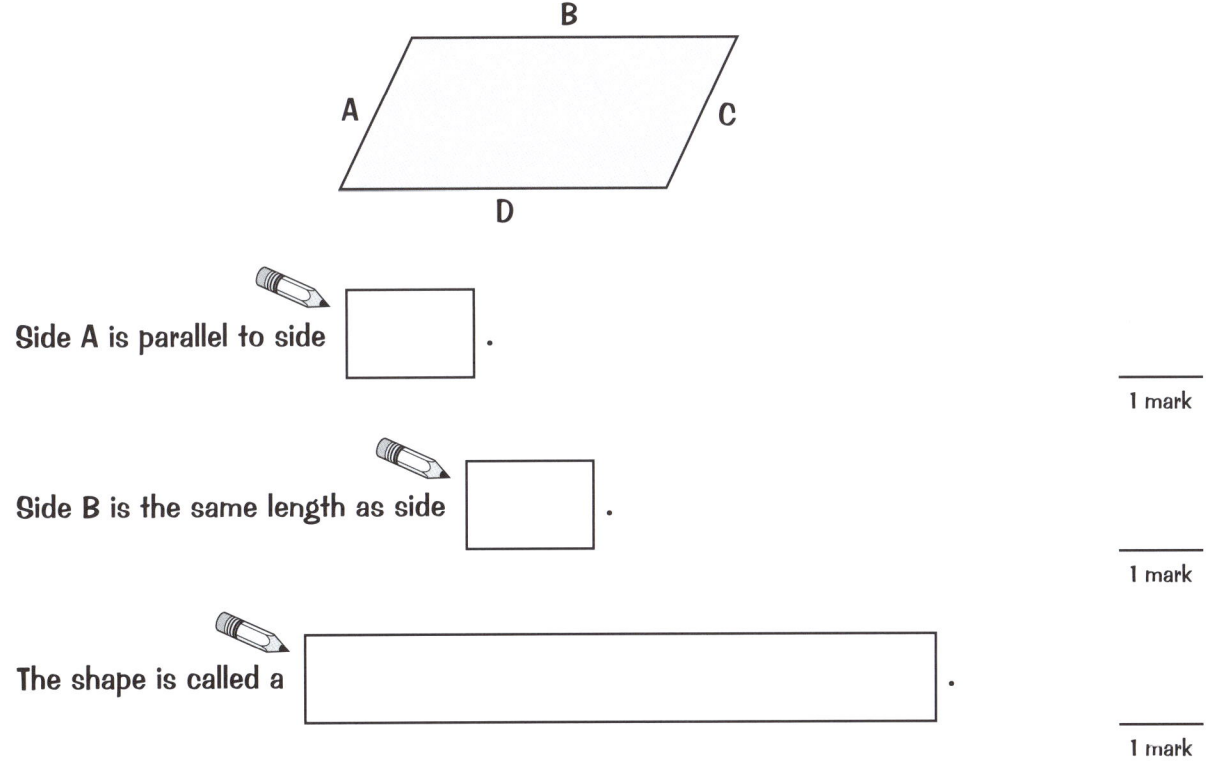

Side A is parallel to side ☐.

1 mark

Side B is the same length as side ☐.

1 mark

The shape is called a ☐.

1 mark

Section Five — Geometry

Comparing Angles

1 Put a tick underneath the **bigger** angle in each box below.

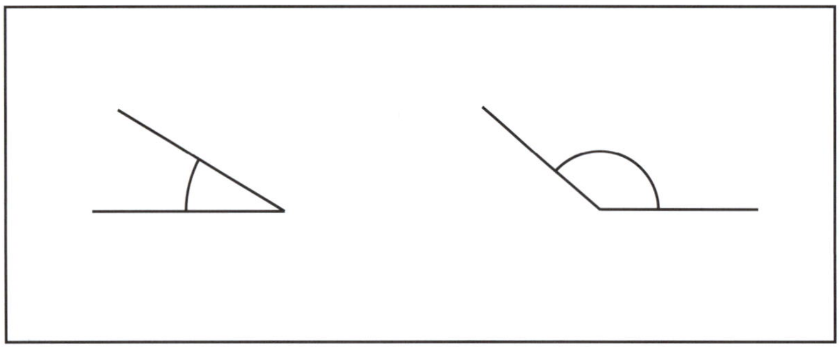

1 mark

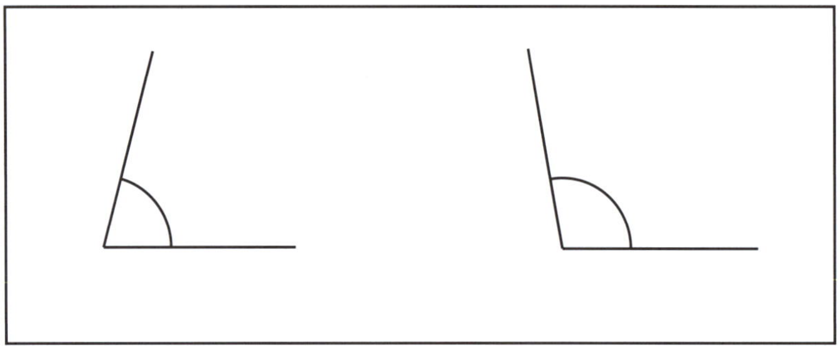

1 mark

2 Look at the three angles below.

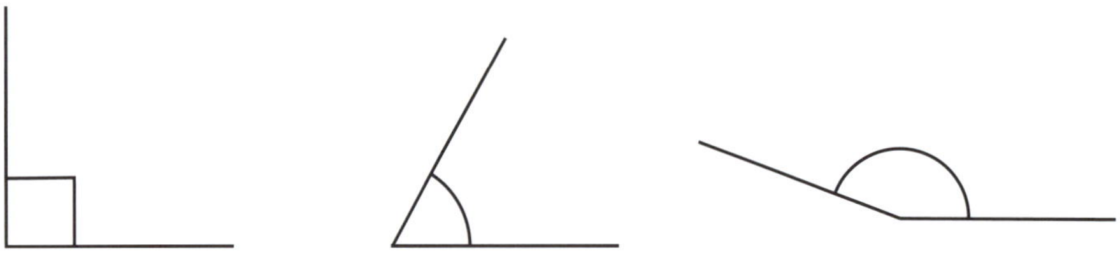

A   B   C

Which is the smallest angle?

1 mark

Which is the largest angle?

1 mark

Section Five — Geometry

Comparing Angles

3 Draw lines to match each angle to the correct name.

right angle   obtuse   acute

2 marks

4 Put these four angles in order, starting with the smallest.

Write the letter of the correct angle in each box.

D   E   F   G

smallest ⟶ largest

1 mark

5 How many acute angles are there in this shape?

1 mark

Section Five — Geometry

Finding Lines of Symmetry

1 Draw all the lines of symmetry on this shape. Use a ruler.

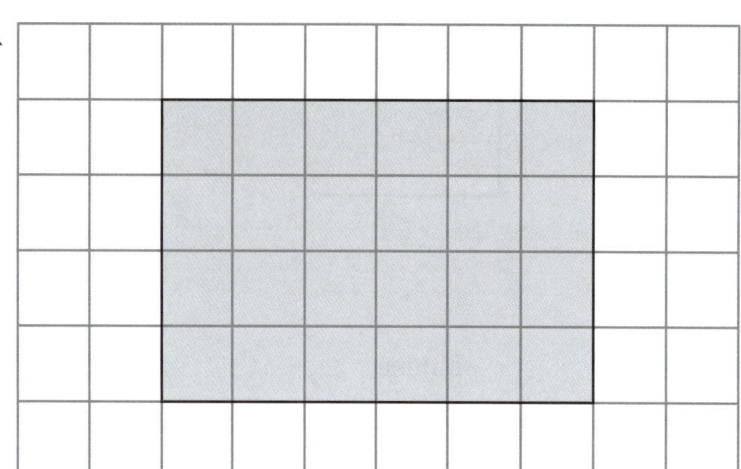

1 mark

2 The three shapes below are equilateral triangles.

Circle the picture that correctly shows all the lines of symmetry.

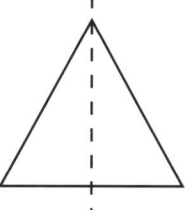 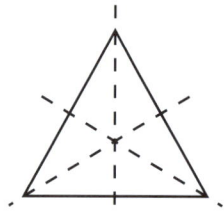 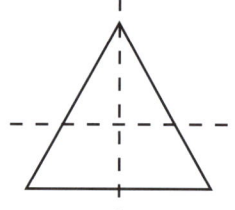

1 mark

3 Draw lines to match each shape to the number of lines of symmetry it has.

One has been done for you.

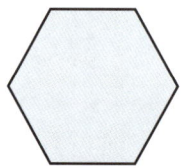  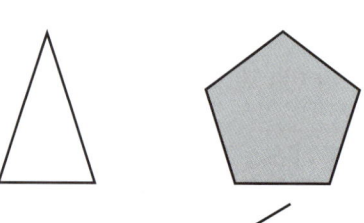

0　　　　1　　　　5　　　　6

2 marks

Section Five — Geometry

Completing Symmetrical Shapes

1 Draw a reflection of this shape in the mirror line. Use a ruler.

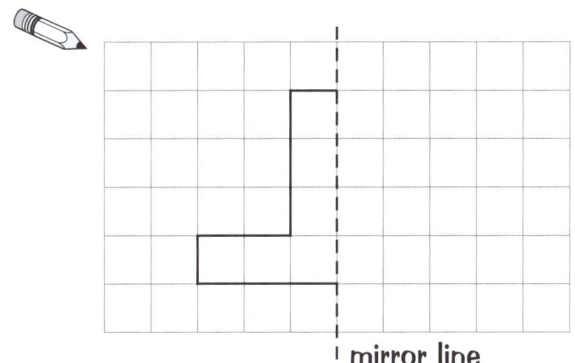

mirror line

1 mark

2 Complete this shape so it is symmetrical in the mirror line. Use a ruler.

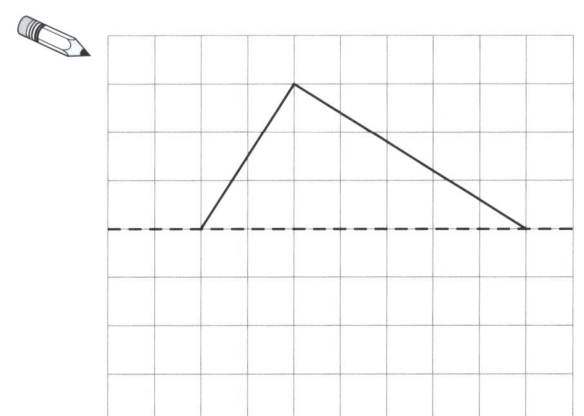

mirror line

1 mark

What is the name of the <u>complete</u> shape you have made?

1 mark

3 Part of a shape has been drawn on this grid.

Complete the shape so it is symmetrical in the mirror line.

Use a ruler.

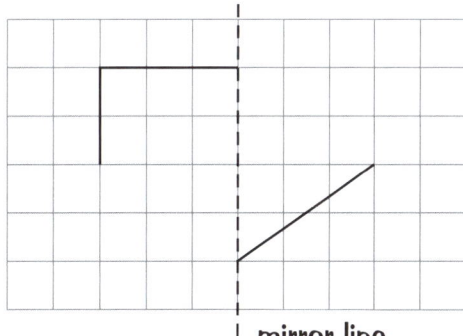

mirror line

1 mark

Section Five — Geometry

Coordinates

1 Some shapes are shown on this grid.

Start at (0, 0).
Count across 5 and up 2.

Draw a ring around the shape you reach.

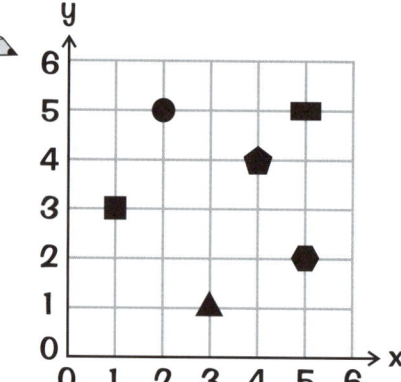

1 mark

2 Some points on this grid are labelled with letters.

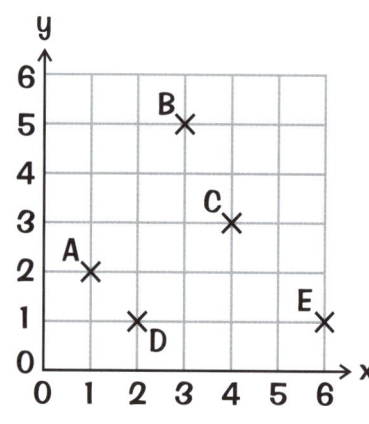

What letter is at (3, 5)?

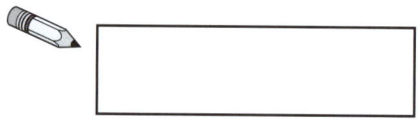

1 mark

What letter is at (1, 2)?

1 mark

3 Five friends stand on a grid on the playground.

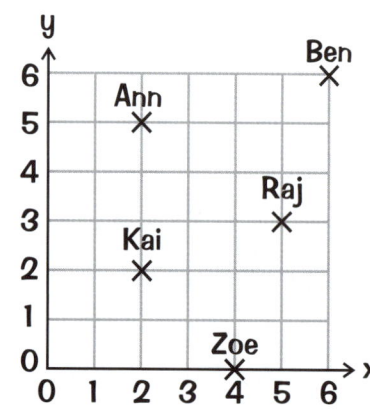

What are Kai's coordinates?

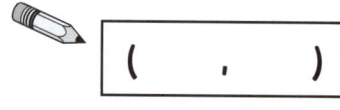

1 mark

What are Zoe's coordinates?

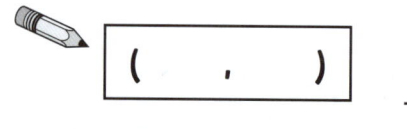

1 mark

Section Five — Geometry

Translations

1 Fill in the boxes to describe how to get from rectangle A to rectangle B.

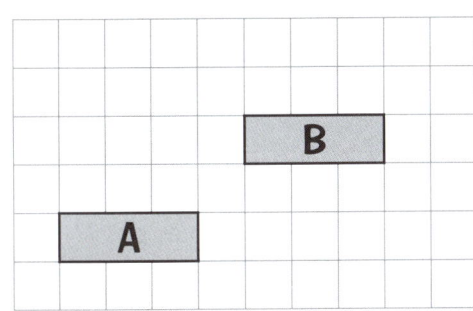
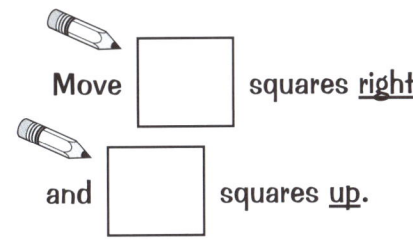

Move ☐ squares right

and ☐ squares up.

1 mark

2 Two triangles are shown on the grid below.

How do you get from triangle P to triangle Q?

Write a number in each box and circle the correct words.

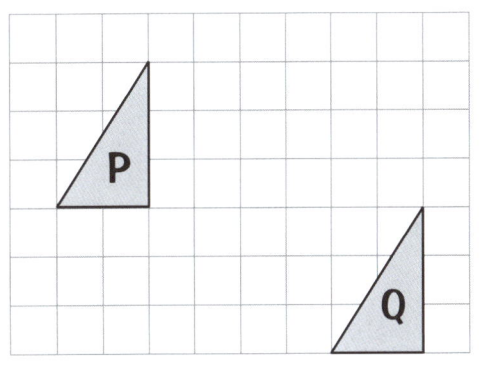

Move ☐ squares right / left

and ☐ squares up / down.

2 marks

3 Fill in the boxes to describe how to translate shape X to get shape Y.

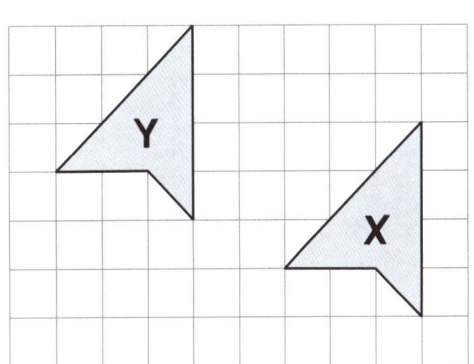

Move ☐ squares _____

and ☐ squares _____ .

2 marks

Section Five — Geometry

Drawing Shapes on Grids

1 Put a cross at (5, 1) on the grid below.
Then join up all the crosses to make a triangle.

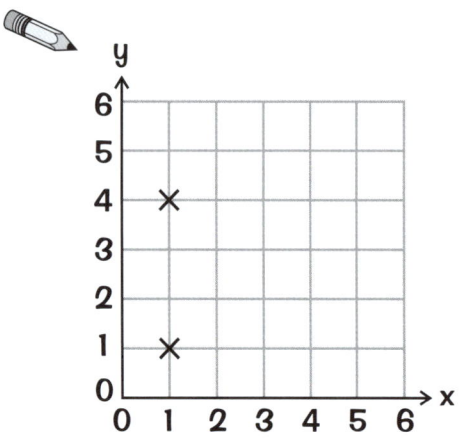

What type of triangle have you made?
Tick the correct box.

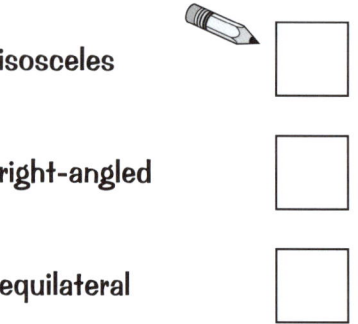

isosceles

right-angled

equilateral

2 marks

2 Put crosses on the grid at these four coordinates.
Then join up the crosses to make a <u>parallelogram</u>.

(1, 1)   (6, 1)

(2, 4)   (7, 4)

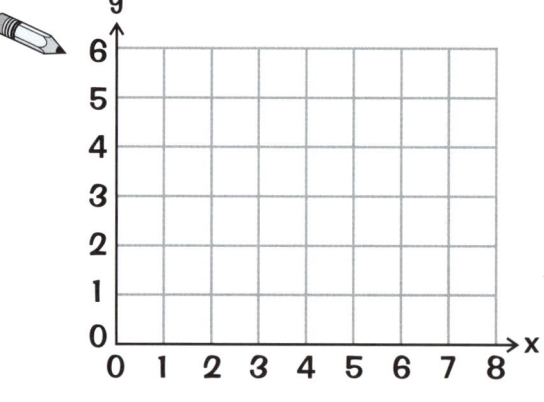

3 marks

3 Three corners of a rectangle have been marked on this grid.

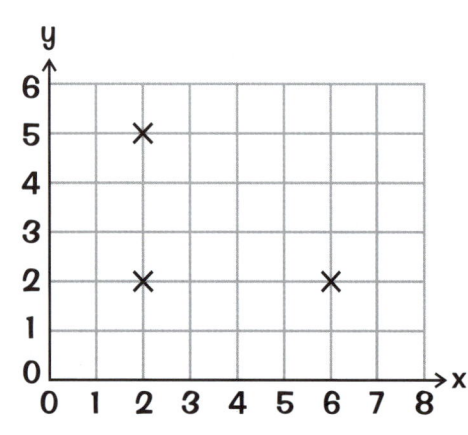

What are the coordinates of the missing corner?

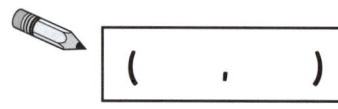

(,)

1 mark

Section Five — Geometry

Section Six — Statistics

Bar Charts

1 Fleur records the number of different owls in a forest. She starts to draw her results in the bar chart below.

There are four more tawny owls than barn owls. Use this information to complete her bar chart.

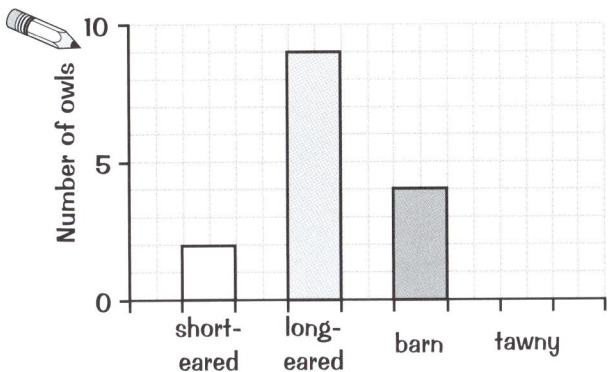

1 mark

Which owl is there the most of?

1 mark

2 Some friends are playing a board game.

The table below shows the number of points each player has.

Player	Number of points
Amy	2
Bill	10
Cody	24
Dessi	16

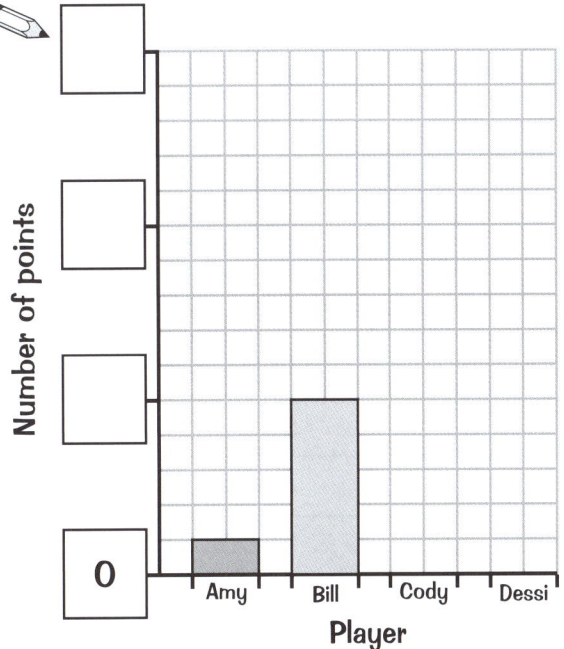

Use the table to fill in the missing numbers on the y-axis and add the missing bars to the chart.

2 marks

Time Graphs

1 Hattie is doing a sponsored walk. She walks 5 km every hour.

Draw a time graph to show this information.
Two points have been drawn for you.

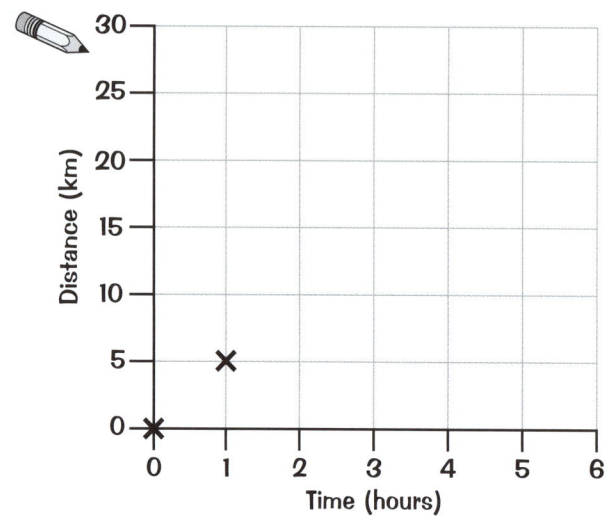

1 mark

2 Sven the snail is in a race.
The distance he has travelled is recorded every minute.

Time (minutes)	Distance (cm)
0	0
1	50
2	150
3	200
4	250
5	350
6	400

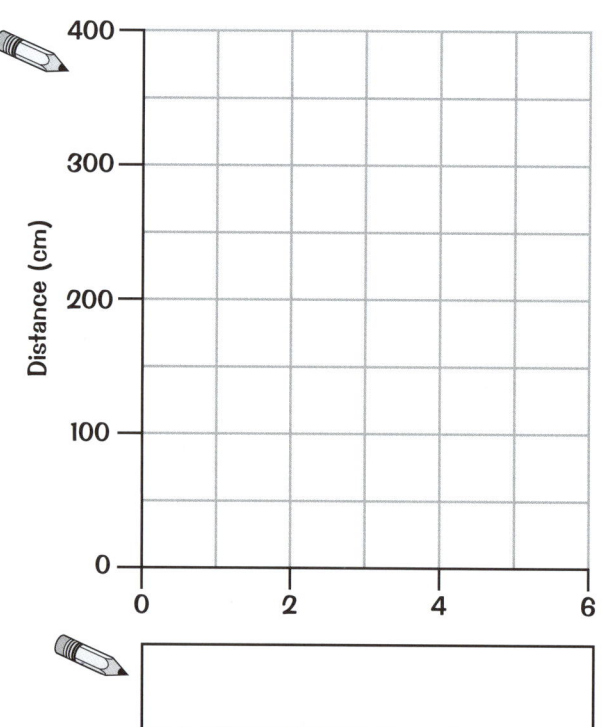

Write the missing label on the horizontal axis of the graph.

1 mark

Use the table to draw a time graph of Sven's race.

1 mark

Section Six — Statistics

Time Graphs

3 A plane sets off at 12 pm.

The time graph shows its height above the ground at different times of the day.

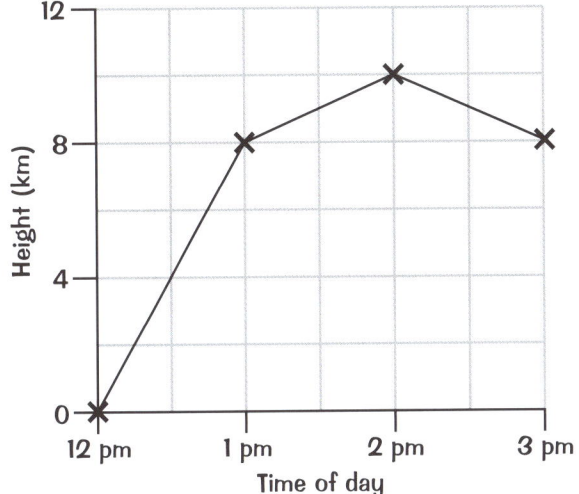

When was the plane at a height of 10 km?

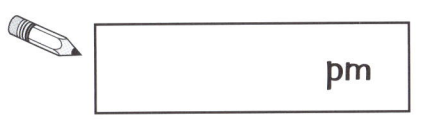

pm

1 mark

What was the difference in the height between 12 pm and 1 pm?

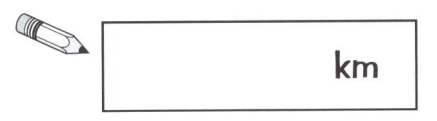

km

1 mark

4 Eric collects rain water in a bowl.
He measures the amount of water in the bowl every 10 minutes.

He plots a time graph of his results.

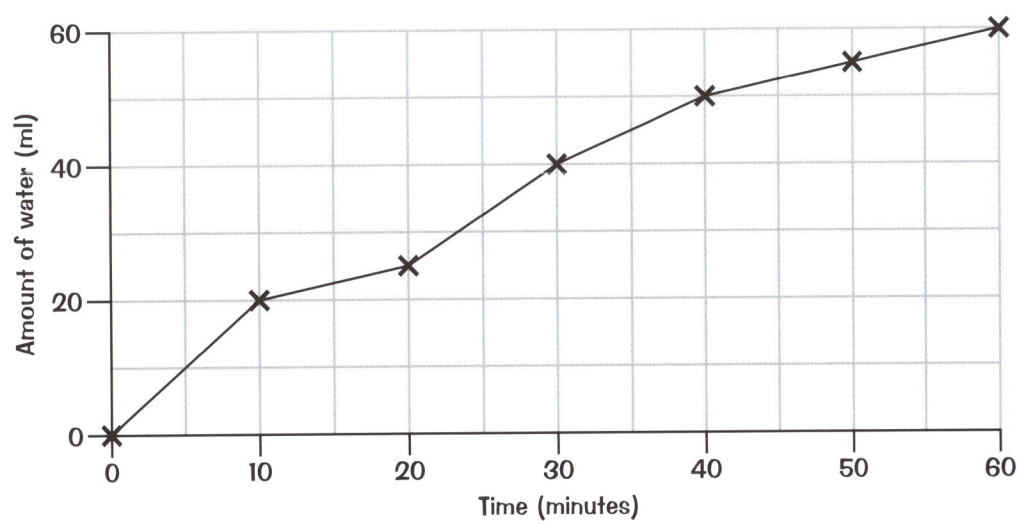

After how many minutes did he record 25 ml of water in the bowl?

minutes

1 mark

How much water was in the bowl after 1 hour?

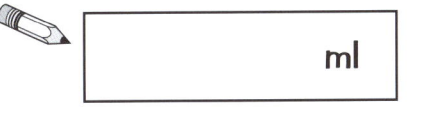

ml

1 mark

Section Six — Statistics

Interpreting Charts and Graphs

1 Four songs were performed at a school talent show.

Each pupil voted for their favourite song.
The results are shown in a bar chart.

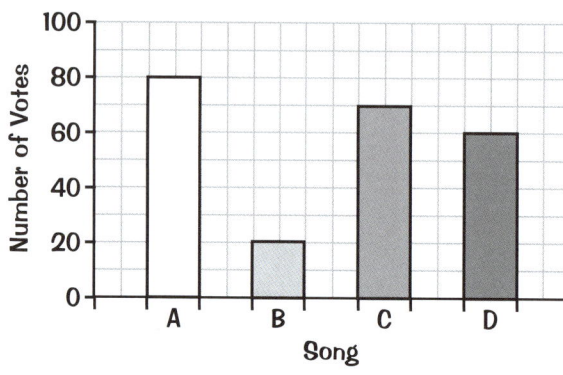

Which song had the fewest votes?

1 mark

How many more pupils voted for Song C than Song D?

pupils

1 mark

2 Three friends are making snowmen.

The pictogram shows the number of snowmen they each make.

How many snowmen does Corey make?

snowmen

1 mark

How many more snowmen does Andy make than Tara?

snowmen

1 mark

Section Six — Statistics

Interpreting Charts and Graphs

3 A Christmas tree starts with 120 working fairy lights.
Ami checks how many working lights there are every 10 hours.

She plots a time graph of her results.

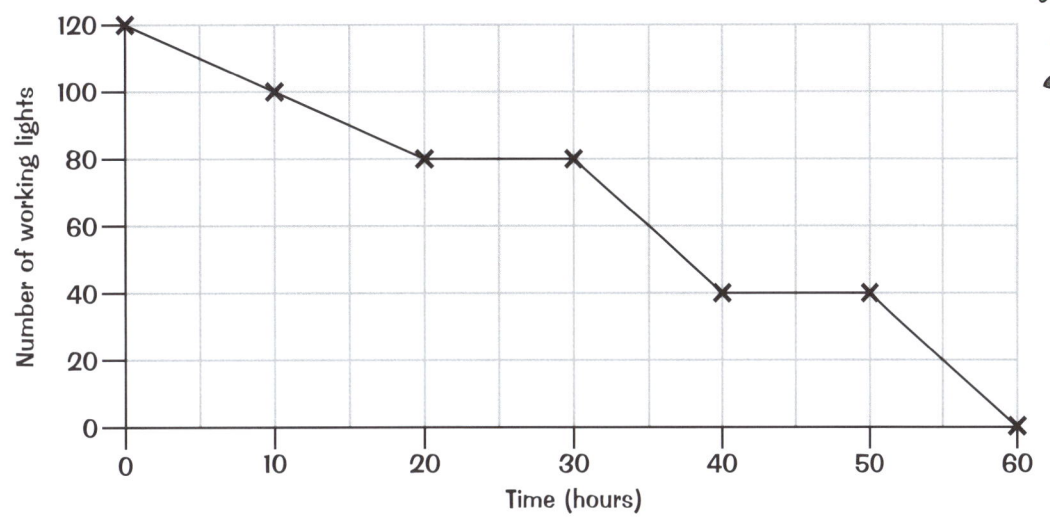

Ami says: "No lights stopped working between 40 and 50 hours."
Do you agree with Ami? Explain your answer.

2 marks

4 Adina and Faye are in the school netball team.

This table shows the number of goals they score in three matches.

	Match 1	Match 2	Match 3
Adina	8	12	6
Faye	11	5	14

In which match did they score 17 goals in total? Circle the correct answer.

  Match 1   Match 2   Match 3

1 mark

How many goals did Faye score in total over the three matches?

 goals

1 mark

Section Six — Statistics

Interpreting Charts and Graphs

5 Sadio records the temperature in his garden on the first day of each month.

The time graph shows his results.

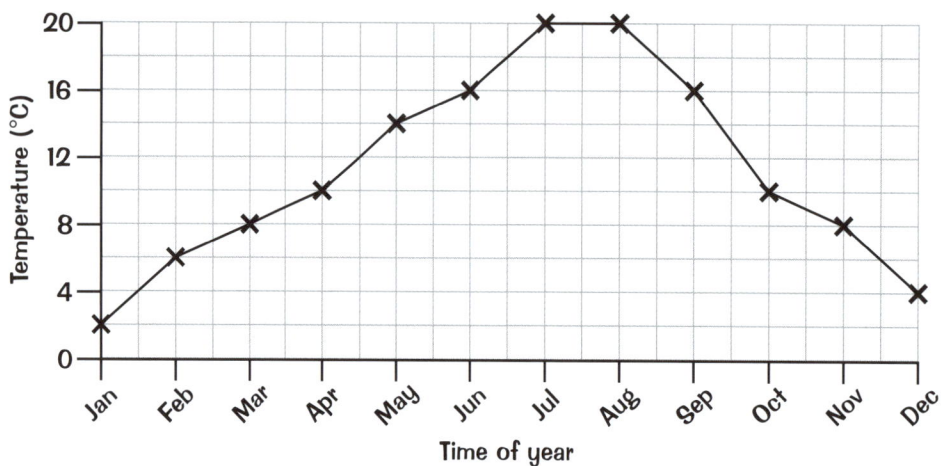

Fill in the boxes to make the sentences correct.

The coldest temperature was recorded in ☐.

1 mark

The temperature was ☐ °C warmer in July than May.

1 mark

6 Cedric sells different bikes in his shop.

This pictogram shows how many 'Goslow' and 'Wuntire' bikes he sold.

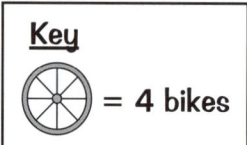

How many 'Goslow' and 'Wuntire' bikes did he sell in total?

☐ bikes

1 mark

He also sold <u>six</u> 'Punkcha' bikes.
How many wheel icons would show this?

☐

1 mark

Section Six — Statistics

Year Four Objectives Test

1) Put these numbers in order. Start with the largest.

   1269   775   1837

   [largest]   [   ]   [smallest]

   1 mark

2) Count forwards in steps of 8 to fill in the boxes.

   [14] , [22] , [   ] , [   ]

   1 mark

3) Dan goes on holiday for 2 weeks and 2 days.

   How many days was Dan on holiday for?

   [   ] days

   1 mark

4) Work out the perimeter of this rectangle.

   7 cm
   4 cm

   [   ] cm

   1 mark

Year Four Objectives Test

Year Four Objectives Test

5) Jane has nine cats. She gives each cat three treats.

How many treats does she give out altogether?

[   ] treats

1 mark

6) Start at 2 and count back 5 steps.

Circle the number you get to on the number line.

–4 –3 –2 –1 0 1 2 3 4

1 mark

7) Fill in the boxes to describe how to get from square M to square N.

Move [   ] squares <u>right</u>

and [   ] squares <u>down</u>.

1 mark

8) What number is shown by the Roman numerals VI?

[   ]

1 mark

9) Circle the best estimate of the answer to 69 + 252.

320   270   350   300

1 mark

Year Four Objectives Test

10) Write the correct names of the angles below.

Use the box of names to help you.

| acute   obtuse   right angle |

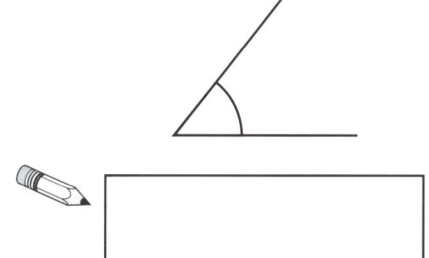
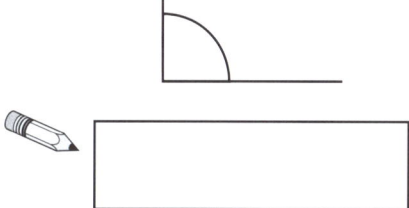

2 marks

11) Calculate:

```
   3 7 6          2 5 4 7
 + 9 2 1        − 1 4 1 8
```

2 marks

12) What is 63 ÷ 1?

Circle the correct answer.

   1   6.3   0   63

1 mark

13) Fill in the missing numbers.

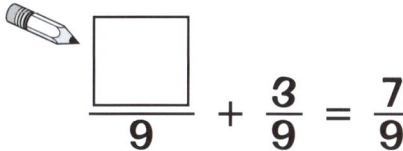

$\frac{\Box}{9} + \frac{3}{9} = \frac{7}{9}$ $\frac{7}{8} + \frac{\Box}{8} = \frac{11}{8}$

2 marks

Year Four Objectives Test

14) Which pentagon shows a correct line of symmetry?

Circle the correct answer.

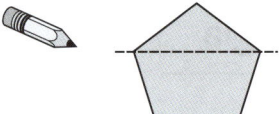 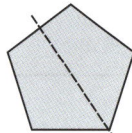 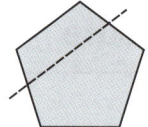

1 mark

15) The bar chart shows the number of hand creams sold by a shop in one day.

Ten rose hand creams were sold.
Use this information to complete the bar chart.

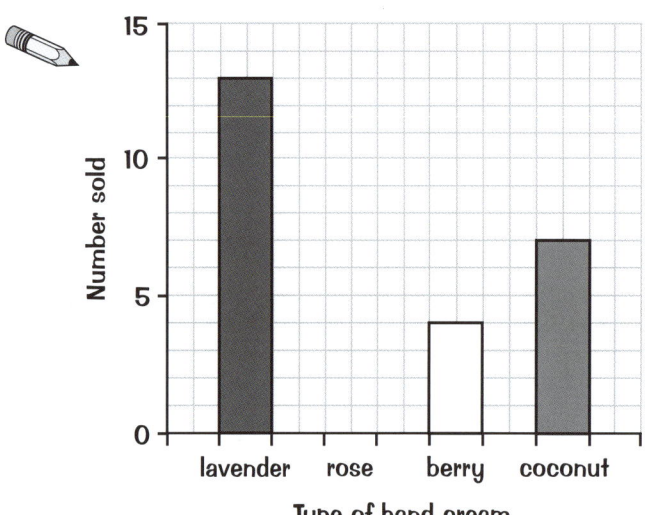

1 mark

What is the total number of hand creams the shop sold?

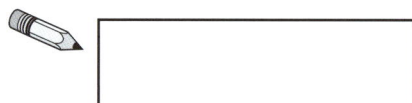

1 mark

16) 10 dominos are stacked on top of each other to make a tower.
The tower is 25 cm high.

What is the height of one domino?

 cm

1 mark

Score: ☐ /20

Answers

Pages 2-5 – Year Three Objectives Test

Q1 12, 16, **20**, **24** *(1 mark)*

Q2 **422** *(1 mark)*
    230 *(1 mark)*

Q3 **three hundred and ninety three** *(1 mark)*

Q4 3 + 3 + 3 = **9 cm** *(1 mark)*

Q5 **12 × 2** and **9 × 3** should be ticked.
    (2 marks for both correct, 1 mark for one correct)

Q6 **5 faces** *(1 mark)*

Q7 712 + 50 = **762** *(1 mark)*
    205 − 20 = **185** *(1 mark)*

Q8 From heaviest to lightest:
    1100 g (Kiwi),
    1 kg (Lime),
    950 g (Strawberry) *(1 mark)*

Q9   1 2 7
    + 3 4 4
      4 7 1
         1 *(1 mark)*

Q10 *(1 mark)*

Q11 2 + 2 = **4 medals** *(1 mark)*

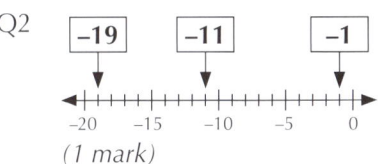
(1 mark)

Q12 E.g.

(1 mark)

Q13 Count from 8:50:
    8:50 → 9:00 → 9:30
    = 10 mins + 30 mins
    = **40 minutes** *(1 mark)*

    3 × 2 = 6 m
    1 m = 100 cm
    6 × 100 = **600 cm** *(1 mark)*

Q14 24 ÷ 3 = 8.
    There are **8 children** in each group. *(1 mark)*

    There are 8 − 3 = 5 children not wearing jumpers in each group.
    So there are 5 × 3
    = **15 children** not wearing jumpers in total. *(1 mark)*

Section One – Number and Place Value

Page 6 – Counting in Multiples

Q1 6, 12, **18**, 24 *(1 mark)*

Q2 25, **50**, 75, 100, **125**
    (1 mark)

Q3   + 1000 + 1000
    2000 3000 4000
    So the answer is **4000**.
    (1 mark)

Q4 **9**, 18, **27**, 36, **45** *(1 mark)*

Q5 **25** and **37** should be circled. *(1 mark)*

Page 7 – Counting Backwards Through Zero

Q1 −6 −5 −4 −3 −2 −1 0
    So the answer is **−6**.
    (1 mark)

Q2 **−19** **−11** **−1**
    (1 mark)

Q3 −4 is **less** than 3. *(1 mark)*
    −2 is **more** than −5. *(1 mark)*

Q4 **−2** *(1 mark)*

Q5 **8 steps** *(1 mark)*

Answers

Page 8 – Place Value and Partitioning

Q1 **1** *(1 mark)*

Q2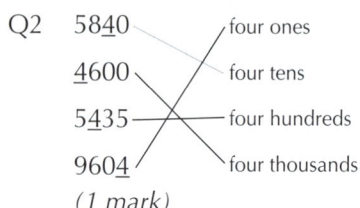
(1 mark)

Q3 2456 = **2000** + **400** + **50** + **6** *(1 mark)*

Q4 **700** or **7 hundreds** *(1 mark)*

Q5 **6061** *(1 mark)*

Page 9 – 1000 More or Less

Q1 **4000** *(1 mark)*

Q2 **8000** *(1 mark)*

Q3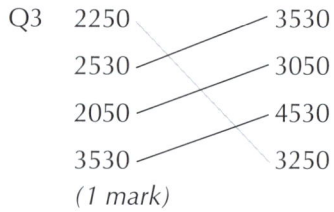
(1 mark)

Q4 **4790** *(1 mark)*

Q5 **154** *(1 mark)*

Pages 10-11 – Ordering and Comparing Numbers

Q1 **8373** and **9500** should be circled. *(1 mark)*

Q2 **2007** and **4780** should be circled. *(1 mark)*

Q3 4580 is **larger** than 580. *(1 mark)*
7512 is **larger** than 6999. *(1 mark)*

Q4 **7880**, **4303**, **900** *(1 mark)*

Q5 **9840** *(1 mark)*

Q6 **Bulb A** *(1 mark)*
Bulb C *(1 mark)*

Q7 **1450**, **1840**, **2450**, **2880** *(1 mark)*

Q8 4510 **<** 8510 *(1 mark)*
7492 **>** 7415 *(1 mark)*

Q9 Either **9998** or **9999**. *(1 mark)*

Pages 12-13 – Rounding

Q1 **10** *(1 mark)*

Q2 42 → **40**
45 → **50**
49 → **50**
(1 mark for all correct)

Q3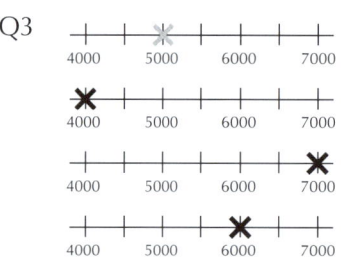
(1 mark for all correct)

Q4 **71** and **67** should be circled. *(1 mark)*

Q5 **500** and **510** *(1 mark)*

Q6 **160** and **230** should be circled. *(1 mark)*

Q7 **2420**, **2400** and **2000** *(1 mark)*

Q8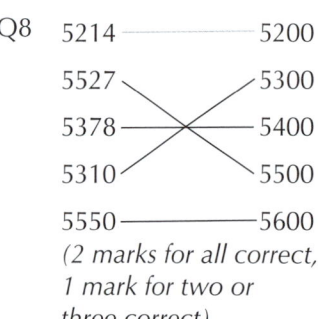
(2 marks for all correct, 1 mark for two or three correct)

Page 14 – Decimal Numbers and Fractions

Q1 $\frac{1}{8}$ *(1 mark)*
$\frac{2}{6}$ *(1 mark)*

Q2 E.g.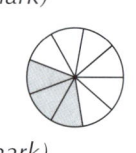
(1 mark)

(1 mark)

Q3 **0.1** *(1 mark)*
3.8 *(1 mark)*

Q4 5 tenths — 0.05
5 hundredths — 5.5
5 ones and 5 tenths — 0.5
(1 mark)

Page 15 – Roman Numerals

Q1 **X** *(1 mark)*

Q2 **100** *(1 mark)*

Q3 XI — 3
III — 6
VI — 60
LI — 51
LX — 11
(2 marks for all correct, 1 mark for two or three correct)

Q4 12 = **XII**
4 = **IV**
24 = **XXIV**
(2 marks for all correct, 1 mark for one or two correct)

Answers

Pages 16-17 – Solving Number Problems

Q1   2500 − 1000 = **1500 m**
(1 mark)

Q2   **75 nuts** *(1 mark)*
25 → **30 nuts** *(1 mark)*

Q3   4287 → **4300**
1455 → **1500**
7120 → **7100**
(1 mark for all correct)

7120 is the largest number so **Flo** got the most points.
(1 mark)

Q4   3 steps of 6 are 18, so **3 trains** go past her.
(1 mark)

Five out of six carriages are full, which is the same as $\frac{5}{6}$.
(1 mark)

Q5   III **<** X and L **>** VI
(1 mark for both correct)

Q6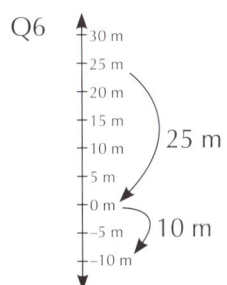

25 + 10 = **35 metres**
(1 mark)

Section Two – Calculations

Page 18 – Written Addition

Q1
```
   5 4 6
 + 4 0 1
 -------
   9 4 7
```
(1 mark)

```
   4 2 4 3
 + 2 0 4 5
 ---------
   6 2 8 8
```
(1 mark)

Q2
```
   2 2 4 7
 + 5 2 1 1
 ---------
   7 4 5 8
```
(1 mark)

Q3
```
   4 5 7 8
 + 4 7 2 1
 ---------
   9 2 9 9
     1
```
(1 mark)

```
   3 5 1 3
 +   4 2 9
 ---------
   3 9 4 2
       1
```
(1 mark)

Q4
```
   9 5 0
 + 3 4 8
 -------
 1 2 9 8
```
(1 mark)

Page 19 – Written Subtraction

Q1
```
   5 8 7
 − 1 5 2
 -------
   4 3 5
```
(1 mark)

```
   5 7 7 9
 − 3 3 6 5
 ---------
   2 4 1 4
```
(1 mark)

Q2
```
   7 5 6
 − 2 4 5
 -------
   5 1 1
```
(1 mark)

Q3
```
   ³4̶ ¹2 8 5
 − 2 7 1 2
 ---------
   1 5 7 3
```
(1 mark)

```
   6 4 ⁵6̶ ¹6
 − 2 1 5 9
 ---------
   4 3 0 7
```
(1 mark)

Q4
```
   8 9 ⁷8̶ ¹4
 −     5 6 8
 -----------
   8 4 1 6
```
(1 mark)

Pages 20-21 – Estimating and Checking

Q1   **66 − 12 = 54** *(1 mark)*

Q2   142 is about **140**.
79 is about **80**.
(1 mark for both correct)
142 + 79 is about
140 + 80 = **220**. *(1 mark)*

Q3   **132** = 95 + 37
or **132** = 37 + **95** *(1 mark)*

Q4   201 + 498 is about
200 + 500 = 700.
So **700** should be circled.
(1 mark)

Q5   65 ÷ 13 = **5**
21 × 4 = **84**
72 ÷ 12 = **6**
(2 marks for all correct, 1 mark for one or two correct)

Q6   52 × 5 is about
50 × 5 = 250. So **250** should be circled. *(1 mark)*

Q7   E.g. the estimate is too high. You can estimate the total with 2 × 20 = **40 g**.
(2 marks — 1 mark for a correct comment about the estimate, 1 mark for 40 g)

Answers

Page 22 – Using Times Tables

Q1 3 × 6 = **18** *(1 mark)*
9 × 6 = **54** *(1 mark)*

Q2 2 × 11 = **22** *(1 mark)*
8 × 11 = **88** *(1 mark)*

Q3 **45**, **18** and **90** should be circled. *(1 mark)*

Q4 3 × 7 = 21 *(1 mark)*
9 × 7 = 63
so 63 ÷ 7 = **9** *(1 mark)*

Q5 4 × 12 = **48 cans** *(1 mark)*

Page 23 – Mental Multiplying and Dividing

Q1 5 × 7 = **35** *(1 mark)*
5 × 70 = **350** *(1 mark)*

Q2 4 × 11 = **44** *(1 mark)*
4 × 11 × 2 = 44 × 2 = **88** *(1 mark)*

Q3 Anything multiplied by zero is zero so **95 × 0** and **0 × 4** should be circled. *(1 mark)*

Q4 53 × 1 = **53** *(1 mark)*
17 ÷ 1 = **17** *(1 mark)*

Q5 60 ÷ 12 = **5 flowers** *(1 mark)*

Page 24 – Factor Pairs

Q1 3 × **4** = 12
2 × **6** = 12
(1 mark for both correct)

Q2
```
      6
1        9
2        3
     18
```
(1 mark)

Q3 **1 and 4**, **2 and 2**
(1 mark for both correct)

Q4 **10 and 6** *(1 mark)*

Q5 **1 × 3** = 3 or **3 × 1** = 3 *(1 mark)*

Page 25 – Written Multiplication

Q1
```
    4 2
  ×   4
　1 6 8
```
(1 mark)

```
    1 4
  ×   7
    9 8
     2
```
(1 mark)

Q2
```
    2 1 3
  ×     3
    6 3 9
```
(1 mark)

```
    1 2 6
  ×     7
    8 8 2
     1 4
```
(1 mark)

Q3
```
    3 4 1
  ×     9
  3 0 6 9
     3
```
(2 marks — 1 mark for attempting to calculate 341 × 9, 1 mark for the correct final answer)

Pages 26-27 – Solving Calculation Problems

Q1
```
  1 3 2 5
+ 7 5 1 2
  8 8 3 7
```
So **8837 cars** crossed the bridge. *(1 mark)*

Q2 6 × 12 = **72 points** *(1 mark)*
12 + 72 = **84 points** *(1 mark)*

Q3
```
  1 ³4̄ ¹4 9
−     3 7 4
  1 0 7 5
```
So the story book has **1075 pages** more. *(1 mark)*

```
  1 4 4 9
+   3 7 4
  1 8 2 3
    1 1
```
So there are **1823 pages** in total. *(1 mark)*

Q4 4 + 3 = 7 magazines in one week.
So 7 × 7 = **49 magazines** in 7 weeks. *(1 mark)*

Q5 2 × 8 = **16 laps** each day *(1 mark)*

```
    1 6
  ×   8
  1 2 8
    4
```
So **128 laps** in eight days.
(2 marks — 1 mark for attempting to multiply their answer by 8, 1 mark for the correct final answer)

Q6 18 ÷ 2 = **9 parks** *(1 mark)*
9 × 5 = **45 swings** *(1 mark)*

Answers

Section Three – Fractions and Decimals

Page 28 – Counting in Hundredths

Q1 $\frac{51}{100}$, $\frac{52}{100}$, $\frac{\mathbf{53}}{\mathbf{100}}$, $\frac{\mathbf{54}}{\mathbf{100}}$
(1 mark)

Q2 $\frac{95}{100}$ — ninety five hundredths
$\frac{2}{100}$ — two hundredths
$\frac{20}{100}$ — twenty hundredths
(1 mark)

Q3 **16 hundredths** *(1 mark)*
19 hundredths *(1 mark)*

Q4 Dividing tenths by 10 gives you hundredths.
So **10 hundredths** will be shaded. *(1 mark)*

Page 29 – Equivalent Fractions

Q1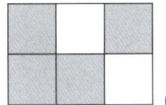
(1 mark)

Q2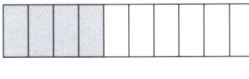
(1 mark)

Q3 **4 parts** *(1 mark)*

Q4 $\frac{\mathbf{4}}{\mathbf{8}}$ and $\frac{\mathbf{5}}{\mathbf{10}}$ should be circled.
(2 marks for both correct, 1 mark for one correct)

Pages 30-31 – Adding and Subtracting Fractions

Q1 E.g.
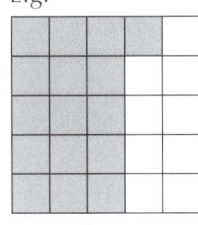
(1 mark)

Q2 $\frac{1}{8} + \frac{4}{8} = \frac{\mathbf{5}}{\mathbf{8}}$ *(1 mark)*
$\frac{6}{10} + \frac{3}{10} = \frac{\mathbf{9}}{\mathbf{10}}$ *(1 mark)*

Q3 E.g.
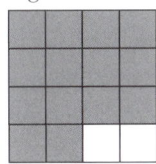
(1 mark)
$\frac{\mathbf{14}}{\mathbf{16}}$ *(1 mark)*

Q4 $\frac{2}{6} + \frac{3}{6} = \frac{\mathbf{5}}{\mathbf{6}}$ *(1 mark)*

Q5 $1 - \frac{2}{5} = \frac{\mathbf{3}}{\mathbf{5}}$ *(1 mark)*

Q6 $\frac{\mathbf{11}}{\mathbf{9}}$ should be circled.
(1 mark)

Q7 $\frac{4}{5} - \frac{\mathbf{1}}{\mathbf{5}} = \frac{3}{5}$ *(1 mark)*
$1 - \frac{\mathbf{2}}{\mathbf{6}} = \frac{4}{6}$ *(1 mark)*

Q8 $\frac{5}{7} + \frac{4}{7} = \frac{\mathbf{9}}{\mathbf{7}}$ *(1 mark)*

Pages 32-33 – Fractions of Amounts

Q1 E.g.
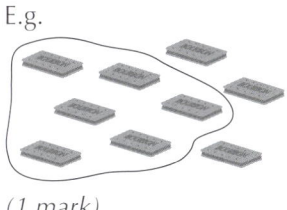
(1 mark)

Q2 E.g.
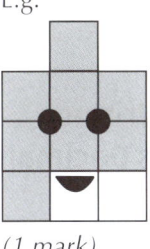
(1 mark)

Q3 $40 \div 5 = \mathbf{8}$ *(1 mark)*

Q4 $\frac{1}{6}$ of 30 = 30 ÷ 6 = 5
So $\frac{2}{6}$ of 30 = 5 × 2 = 10
So **10** should be circled.
(1 mark)

Q5 $\frac{1}{4}$ of 16 is 16 ÷ 4 = **4**, so
$\frac{3}{4}$ of 16 is 3 × 4 = **12**
(1 mark)

$\frac{1}{10}$ of 50 is
50 ÷ 10 = **5**, so
$\frac{7}{10}$ of 50 = 7 × 5 = **35**
(1 mark)

Q6 $\frac{1}{10}$ of 100 is
100 ÷ 10 = 10,
so $\frac{4}{10}$ of 100 is
10 × 4 = **40** *(1 mark)*

Q7 $\frac{1}{3}$ of 27 is 27 ÷ 3 = 9, so
$\frac{2}{3}$ of 27 is 9 × 2 = 18.
So there are **18 teddy bears**.
(1 mark)

Q8 $\frac{1}{5}$ of 35 = 35 ÷ 5 = 7
35 − 7 = **28** *(1 mark)*

Answers

Page 34 – Decimals

Q1 **5 tenths** *(1 mark)*
5 hundredths *(1 mark)*

Q2 **4.5** *(1 mark)*
5.7 *(1 mark)*

Q3 **0.21** should be circled. *(1 mark)*

Q4 **4.6** *(1 mark)*
7.38 *(1 mark)*

Page 35 – Writing Fractions as Decimals

Q1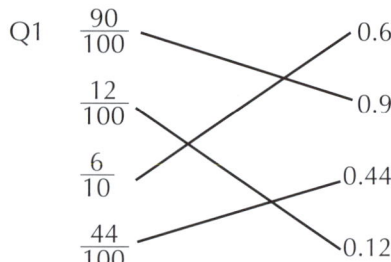

(2 marks for all correct, 1 mark for two or three correct)

Q2 **0.08** *(1 mark)*

Q3 **0.25** should be circled. *(1 mark)*

Q4 **0.5** *(1 mark)*
0.75 *(1 mark)*

Pages 36-37 – Dividing by 10 and 100

Q1 **5**, **6.8** *(1 mark)*
3.7, **0.9** *(1 mark)*

Q2 **8.1** should be circled. *(1 mark)*

Q3 **0.26** should be circled. *(1 mark)*

Q4 93 ÷ 100 = **0.93** *(1 mark)*

Q5 40 ÷ 10 = **4 pieces** *(1 mark)*

Q6 32 ÷ 100 = **0.32 kg** *(1 mark)*

Q7 0.2 0.9 1.7 on number line 0 to 3

(2 marks for all correct, 1 mark for one or two correct)

Q8 0.8 × 10 = 8, so **8** should be circled. *(1 mark)*

Page 38 – Rounding Decimals

Q1 **51** *(1 mark)*
52 *(1 mark)*

Q2 **7, 15**
9, 31
(2 marks for all correct, 1 mark for two or three correct)

Q3 **4 m** should be circled. *(1 mark)*

Q4 **100** *(1 mark)*

Page 39 – Comparing Decimals

Q1 **23.7** should be circled. *(1 mark)*

Q2 **6.1**, **6.5**, **7.2** *(1 mark)*

Q3 **B** *(1 mark)*

Q4 **£2.85, £3.15, £3.35, £3.50** *(1 mark)*

Pages 40-41 – Solving Fraction and Decimal Problems

Q1 $\frac{1}{8} + \frac{5}{8} = \frac{6}{8}$ *(1 mark)*

Q2 46 ÷ 10 = 4.6, so **£4.60** should be circled. *(1 mark)*

Q3 $1 - \frac{5}{6} = \frac{6}{6} - \frac{5}{6} = \frac{1}{6}$ *(1 mark)*

Q4 $\frac{2}{4}$, $\frac{1}{2}$ and $\frac{6}{12}$ should be circled.
(2 marks for all correct, 1 mark for one or two correct)

Q5 **D** *(1 mark)*
C *(1 mark)*

Q6 3.8 + 0.1 + 0.1 + 0.1 + 0.1 = **4.2 m** *(1 mark)*

4 m *(1 mark)*

Q7 $\frac{1}{4}$ of £24 is £24 ÷ 4 = £6
$\frac{3}{4}$ of £24 is 3 × £6 = £18
£24 − £18 = **£6**. *(1 mark)*

Answers

Section Four – Measurement

Pages 42-43 – Units

Q1 1 kg = 1000 g
2 × 1000 = **2000 g** *(1 mark)*

1 litre = 1000 ml
4 × 1000 = **4000 ml**
(1 mark)

Q2 [35 mm] [68 mm] *(1 mark)*

Q3 1 hour = 60 minutes
3 × 60 = 180.
180 should be circled.
(1 mark)

Q4 5 m — 50 cm
5 km — 5000 m
0.5 km — 500 m
0.5 m — 500 cm
(2 marks for all correct, 1 mark for two correct)

Q5 1.3 m = 130 cm,
125 is less than 130 and 135, so **Tonya** is the shortest. *(1 mark)*

Q6 8 litres = 8000 ml
0.5 litres = 500 ml
So 8000 + 500 = **8500 ml**
(1 mark)

Q7 Parcel A = 1.2 × 1000
= 1200 g
Parcel B = 1500 g
Parcel B is 1500 − 1200
= **300 g** heavier. *(1 mark)*

Pages 44-45 – Perimeter

Q1 3 + 3 + 3 + 3 = **12 cm**
(1 mark)

10 + 10 + 10 + 10
= **40 cm** *(1 mark)*

Q2 10 + 1 + 10 + 1 = 22 cm.
22 cm should be circled.
(1 mark)

Q3 6 + 3 + 6 + 3 = **18 cm**
(1 mark)

Q4 200 + 50 + 200 + 50
= **500 cm** *(1 mark)*

Q5 4 + 4 + 4 + 4 = 16 m.
4 m should be circled.
(1 mark)

Q6 Shape A:
5 + 3 + 5 + 3 = 16 cm
Shape B:
9 + 1 + 9 + 1 = 20 cm
The perimeter of B is
20 − 16 = **4 cm** longer.
(2 marks — 1 mark for finding the correct perimeter of at least one shape, 1 mark for the correct final answer)

Pages 46-47 – Area

Q1 **6 squares** *(1 mark)*

Q2 **6 cm², 9 cm², 10 cm², 10 cm²**
(2 marks for all correct, 1 mark for two or three correct)

Q3 **Shape B** should be circled.
(1 mark)

Shape C should be circled.
(1 mark)

Q4 E.g.

(1 mark for a shape made up of 14 shaded squares)

Pages 48-49 – Money

Q1 80 + 40 = 120p = **£1.20**
(1 mark)

£1.50 + £0.55 = **£2.05**
(1 mark)

130 − 60 = 70p = **£0.70**
(1 mark)

220 − 20 − 10 = 190p
= **£1.90** *(1 mark)*

Q2 210 × 2 = 420p = **£4.20**
(1 mark)

Q3 312 − 50 = 262p = **£2.62**
(1 mark)

Q4 180 ÷ 3 = 60p = £0.60.
£0.60 should be circled.
(1 mark)

Q5 The **Rat** card should be circled. *(1 mark)*

21 + 19 = 40p
100 − 40 = 60p = **£0.60**
(1 mark)

Q6 180 + 150 = 330p
115 + 200 = 315p
330p is bigger than 315p, so **piggy bank A** has more money.
(2 marks — 1 mark for a correct method, 1 mark for the correct answer)

Answers

Page 50 – Clocks

Q1 **twenty-two minutes past eleven** *(1 mark)*

Q2 **2:30 pm** *(1 mark)*
8:45 pm *(1 mark)*

Q3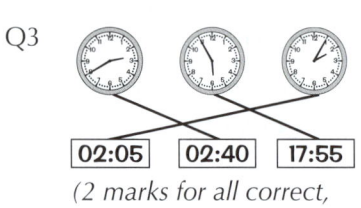
(2 marks for all correct, 1 mark for one or two correct)

Q4 **15:32** *(1 mark)*

Page 51 – Time Problems

Q1 1 week = **7 days**, so 3 weeks
= 3 × **7**
= **21** days
(1 mark for all correct)

Q2 1 year = 12 months
12 + 6 = **18 months**
(1 mark)

Q3 Count on from 6:00:
6:00 → 8:00 → 8:15
= 2 hours + 15 minutes
= **135 minutes** *(1 mark)*

Q4 1 minute = 60 seconds
3 minutes and 5 seconds
= 180 + 5 = 185 seconds.
She ran for 185 + 200
= **385 seconds**. *(1 mark)*

Section Five – Geometry

Pages 52-53 – Comparing 2D Shapes

Q1 The shapes and names should be matched up like this:

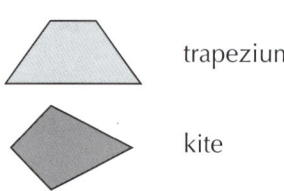

(2 marks for all correct, 1 mark for one or two correct)

Q2 E.g.

(1 mark)

Q3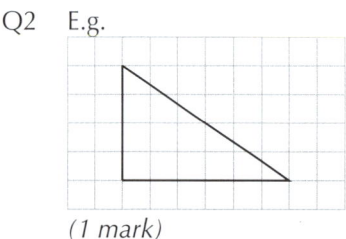
(1 mark)

Q4 Triangle **3** is equilateral.
Triangle **2** is isosceles.
Triangle **1** is scalene.
(2 marks for all correct, 1 mark for one or two correct)

Q5 Side A is parallel to side **C**. *(1 mark)*
Side B is the same length as side **D**. *(1 mark)*
The shape is called a **parallelogram**. *(1 mark)*

Pages 54-55 – Comparing Angles

Q1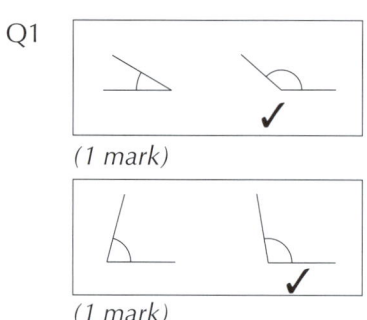
(1 mark)

(1 mark)

Q2 **B** *(1 mark)*
C *(1 mark)*

Q3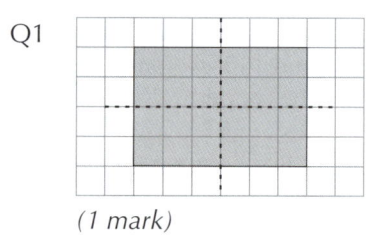
(2 marks for all correct, 1 mark for at least one correct)

Q4 **EGFD** *(1 mark)*

Q5 **2** *(1 mark)*

Page 56 – Finding Lines of Symmetry

Q1
(1 mark)

Q2
(1 mark)

Q3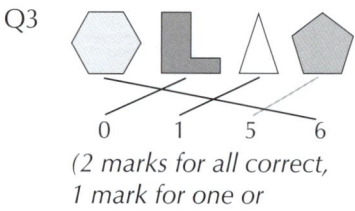
(2 marks for all correct, 1 mark for one or two correct)

Answers

Page 57 – Completing Symmetrical Shapes

Q1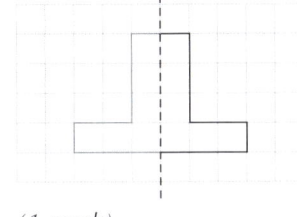
(1 mark)

Q2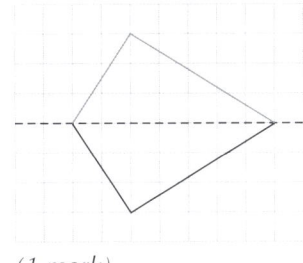
(1 mark)
kite *(1 mark)*

Q3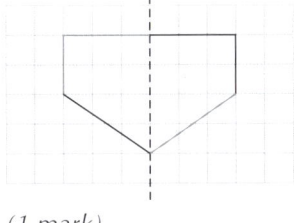
(1 mark)

Page 58 – Coordinates

Q1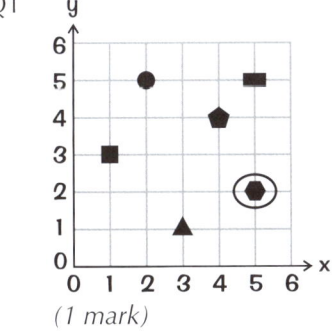
(1 mark)

Q2 **B** *(1 mark)*
A *(1 mark)*

Q3 **(2, 2)** *(1 mark)*
(4, 0) *(1 mark)*

Page 59 – Translations

Q1 Move **4** squares **right** and **2** squares **up**. *(1 mark)*

Q2 Move **6** squares **right** *(1 mark)* and **3** squares **down** *(1 mark)*.

Q3 Move **5** squares **left** *(1 mark)* and **2** squares **up** *(1 mark)*.

Page 60 – Drawing Shapes on Grids

Q1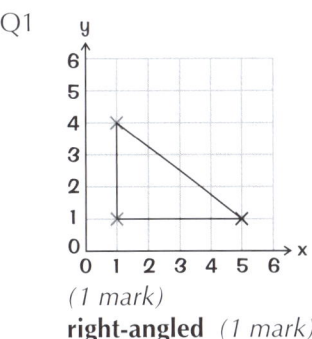
(1 mark)
right-angled *(1 mark)*

Q2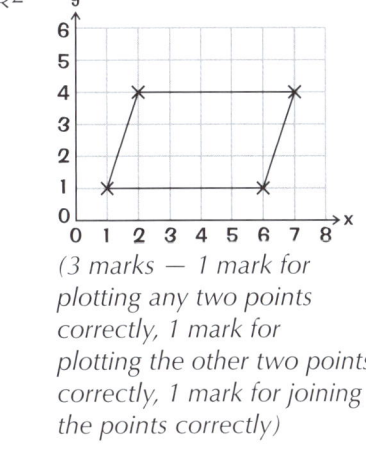
(3 marks — 1 mark for plotting any two points correctly, 1 mark for plotting the other two points correctly, 1 mark for joining the points correctly)

Q3 **(6, 5)** *(1 mark)*

Section Six – Statistics

Page 61 – Bar Charts

Q1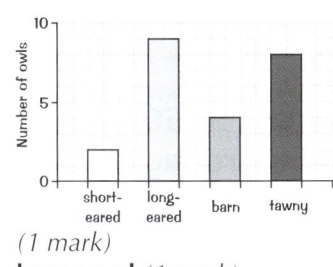
(1 mark)
long-eared *(1 mark)*

Q2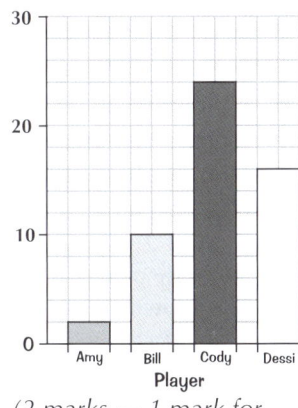
(2 marks — 1 mark for the correct scale, 1 mark for all the bars correct)

Pages 62-63 – Time Graphs

Q1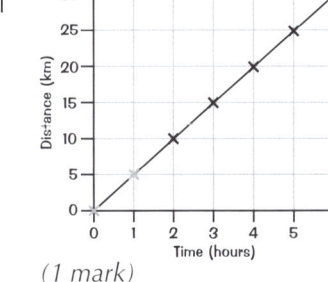
(1 mark)

Q2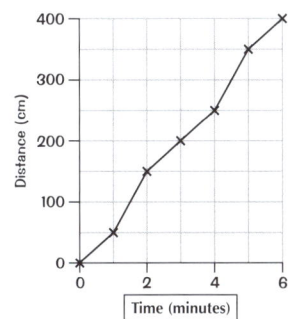
(2 marks — 1 mark for correct label, 1 mark for correctly plotted points joined by straight lines)

Answers

Q3 **2 pm** *(1 mark)*
8 − 0 = **8 km** *(1 mark)*

Q4 **20 minutes** *(1 mark)*
60 ml *(1 mark)*

Pages 64-66 – Interpreting Charts and Graphs

Q1 **Song B** *(1 mark)*
70 − 60 = **10 pupils**
(1 mark)

Q2 2 + 2 + 2 + 2 = **8 snowmen**
(1 mark)
Andy:
2 + 2 + 2 + 2 + 2 = 10
Tara:
2 + 2 + 2 + 1 = 7
So Andy makes 10 − 7
= **3 snowmen** more.
(1 mark)

Q3 **Yes** — there were 40 working lights after 40 hours and after 50 hours, so no lights stopped working between these times.
(2 marks — 1 mark for the correct answer, 1 mark for an explanation)

Q4 12 + 5 = 17, so **Match 2** should be circled.
(1 mark)
11 + 5 + 14 = **30 goals**
(1 mark)

Q5 The coldest temperature was recorded in **January**.
(1 mark)
The temperature was **6 °C** warmer in July than May.
(1 mark)

Q6 One quarter of a wheel icon is worth 1 bike.
3 whole and 1 quarter icons
= 4 + 4 + 4 + 1
= **13 bikes**. *(1 mark)*
One half of a wheel icon is worth 2 bikes.
1 whole and 1 half ($1\frac{1}{2}$) icons = 4 + 2 = 6 bikes.
(1 mark)

Pages 67-70 – Year Four Objectives Test

Q1 From largest to smallest:
1837, **1269**, **775** *(1 mark)*

Q2 14, 22, **30**, **38** *(1 mark)*

Q3 1 week = 7 days,
2 weeks = 2 × 7 = 14 days
14 + 2 = **16 days** *(1 mark)*

Q4 7 + 4 + 7 + 4 = **22 cm**
(1 mark)

Q5 9 × 3 = **27 treats** *(1 mark)*

Q6
```
-4 (-3) -2 -1  0  1  2  3  4
```
(1 mark)

Q7 Move **5 squares right** and **3 squares down** *(1 mark)*

Q8 **6** *(1 mark)*

Q9 70 + 250 = **320** *(1 mark)*

Q10 **acute** *(1 mark)*
right angle *(1 mark)*

Q11
```
   3 7 6
 + 9 2 1
  1 2 9 7
```
(1 mark)
```
  2 5 ³4̸ 7
 −1 4 1 8
  1 1 2 9
```
(1 mark)

Q12 **63** *(1 mark)*

Q13 $\frac{4}{9} + \frac{3}{9} = \frac{7}{9}$ *(1 mark)*
$\frac{7}{8} + \frac{4}{8} = \frac{11}{8}$ *(1 mark)*

Q14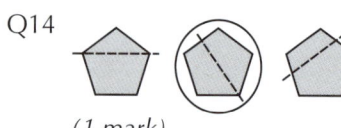
(1 mark)

Q15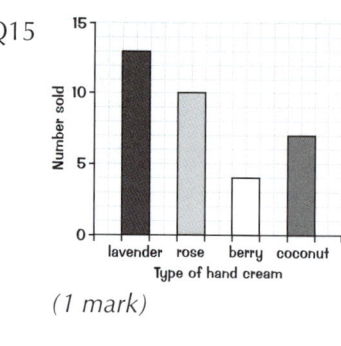
(1 mark)
13 + 10 + 4 + 7 = 34
(1 mark)

Q16 10 dominos are 25 cm high, so 1 domino is 25 ÷ 10 = **2.5 cm** high. *(1 mark)*